LOUIS MACNEICE

Louis MacNeice by Nancy Sharp, 1937.

Louis MacNeice

In A Between World

CHRISTOPHER J. FAUSKE

IRISH ACADEMIC PRESS

First published in 2016 by
Irish Academic Press
8 Chapel Lane
Sallins
Co. Kildare
Ireland

© Christopher J. Fauske 2016

British Library Cataloguing-in-Publication Data:
An entry can be found on request.

ISBN: 978-1-911024-09-5 (paper)
ISBN: 978-1-911024-10-1 (cloth)
ISBN: 978-1-911024-11-8 (PDF)
ISBN: 978-1-911024-12-5 (Epub)
ISBN: 978-1-911024-13-2 (Kindle)

Library of Congress Cataloging-in-Publication Data:
An entry can be found on request.

Contents

Author Note

References to the poems of Louis MacNeice are as they appear in *Collected Poems*, ed. Peter McDonald (London: Faber, 2007) except as noted. References to Louis MacNeice's correspondence are to the *Letters of Louis MacNeice*, ed. Jonathan Allison (London: Faber, 2010) except as noted.

Throughout this book I have silently altered grammar and spelling in the letters and notes of MacNeice. He did not intend them for publication so his grammar is idiosyncratic and his spelling is occasionally wayward in many of them. I have on a few occasions silently corrected obvious typos in other people's published work.

Generally, female contemporaries of MacNeice are referred to by their maiden names in order not to confuse the reader when the women marry or re-marry. The exception is Louis's sister, Elizabeth, who is most often referred to by her married name, Nicholson.

References to the Bible are to the King James Version. The dates of BBC broadcasts have been confirmed where possible in multiple sources, but I have relied, ultimately, on the BBC Genome Project – http://genome.ch.bbc.co.uk/.

ACKNOWLEDGEMENTS

Invaluable advice and research assistance was provided by C. Ivar McGrath, Marnie Hay and Patrick Walsh. Nancy Dennis and Rebecca LeMonat at Salem State University Library, as well as librarians at the Birmingham University Libraries, the New York Public Library and the University of Delaware Library all answered research questions with patience and insight. I thank them for their professionalism, courtesy and unstinting efforts to track down obscure snippets of information.

Partial funding for the development of this book was provided by the Salem State University Research Advisory Committee. At Irish Academic Press, Lisa Hyde always proved an encouraging advisor and helped shape this book for the better. I would also like to thank Kaye Coates at the Woodland Trust (Northern Ireland).

As well as providing the foreword, James Ward encouraged me to revisit Louis MacNeice when we met at a conference on eighteenth-century matters. I am grateful to him for listening to me at length as I thought about the project.

Permission to quote from the poetry, prose and drama of Louis MacNeice was provided by David Higham Associates. Permission to quote from the unpublished correspondence of Nancy Sharp and to reproduce the sketch of Louis MacNeice in the Hebrides was granted by Philip Spender on behalf of her estate. The National Library of Scotland digitised the sketch for reproduction.

Foreword

Louis MacNeice's life and work offer a sceptical, sidelong perspective on his times. His inheritance was worn ambivalently in a context of enquiry and transformation, a legacy both of his upbringing and of his sense of dislocation from various possible 'homes'. MacNeice's rectory childhood provided more than what the poem 'Carrick Revisited' calls 'a topographical frame'.[1] His birth 'between the mountain and the gantries'[2] placed him on the edge of both tradition and modernity, and borders and between-ness run through his work like a watermark. His boundaries were mutable rather than fixed. If in the early twentieth century Ireland was a concept, as this study indicates, 'whose meaning shifted across geography and economics and religion', MacNeice was surely not alone in wondering where he would wake up each morning, and so one of his defining attributes was a sense of an 'imperative to look beyond, not past, the contemporary world'.

There was also a turning point at the age of seven which meant that 'Nothing after was quite the same.'[3] MacNeice's childhood, as he reconstructed it, was a narrative of displacement and dislocation, a sense of separateness mixed with a wariness about belonging that continued throughout his life. Although it would not be so unusual in a writer born around the same time in continental Europe, MacNeice's conscious adoption in adulthood of culturally and nationally ambiguous identities makes him unique among modern Irish poets.

Others continue to seek identity on MacNeice's behalf. The 'rage for order'[4] of the critic-taxonomists has tagged MacNeice as both the last Anglo-Irish and the first Northern Irish poet, although he never thought of himself as either. The latter description, in particular, holds special resonance for those critics and poets who came of age around the time of MacNeice's death and had the need for identity thrust upon them with the resurgence of political violence in the late 1960s. It has become a truism to say that MacNeice's reputation suffered after his death and even before it – the bright young 1930s poet adrift first in the post-war period and then in postmodernity. But in violent times his work with its emphasis on the personal in the face of the public was appreciated with a new urgency. It is not hard to see why MacNeice became talismanic in this context.

His ethos of lyrical doubt can be seen and heard in Tom Paulin's mix of demotic and philosophical registers, in the long, questing lines of Ciaran Carson and in the rueful, studied cosmopolitanism of Derek Mahon. MacNeice's importance in Northern contexts endures beyond the 1960s' generation: Tyrone-reared poet Nick Laird describes reading MacNeice's work in the 1980s and early 1990s as 'contemporary commentary on what we were then living through'.[5] But as the cataclysm subsides a new sense of MacNeice's place in the world emerges. Described by John Kerrigan as a truly archipelagic poet, MacNeice was a seeker of island life who now helps embody the plurality and totality of relations between our islands – for MacNeice made 'between' into a word that separates as it joins.[6]

As the twentieth century recedes from view, MacNeice seems more and differently political than he was allowed to be in his own time. Writing in 1998, Terence Brown found in his poetry a corrective to the neo-liberal economic savagery of the Thatcherite project, while Alan Gillis has more recently shown how the poetry of the 1950s 'bore witness to the loss of collective energy' and 'decline of communality' as people on both sides of the Irish Sea 'floundered … towards a consumerist society'.[7] MacNeice's critique was, however, dismissive only of those forms of consumption degrading to the individual. His poems' pleasurable immersions in a world of objects, goods and things amply testify to his delight in the material world, moving beyond a mere keenness of observation. Mockingly grouped among the 'pylon boys',[8] MacNeice is more correctly identified as a laureate of nylon stockings and train carriages, of wallpaper and budgie cages, of barometers and cigarettes.

Consumption came at a price nonetheless: The 'blue smoke rising and the brown lace sinking | In the glass of stout'[9] left 'Lungs that are black, tongues that are dry'.[10] MacNeice's materialism resembles that of Gerard Manley Hopkins, another, more tortured, sensualist, whom he praised for 'zeal in recording the visions of the bodily eye'.[11] His own epiphanic outburst 'Snow' goes three better, recording impressions felt not just visually but 'On the tongue on the eyes on the ears in the palms of one's hands'.[12] But 'the drunkenness of things being various'[13] can slide from the camaraderie of what the poem 'Alcohol' calls 'a factitious popular front' into alienated isolation.[14] Often, the tipping point is recollection. The poem 'When we were children' describes spring 'scrambling the laburnum tree – | A breakfast for the gluttonous eye',[15] while, in 'Carrick Revisited', 'a child in bed | Glimpses a brangle of talk from the floor below'.[16] Undercutting the initial rush of sensation are the facts that the yellow flowers of the laburnum tree are poisonous and that the word 'brangle', though delightful to the ear, connotes quarrelsome disputation. Memory, like politics, was for MacNeice a process of estrangement.

Both were rooted in a metaphysics which balanced glittering surfaces against a quest to see 'what stalks behind'.[17] This worldview brought together materialist and mystical perspectives, embracing their dissonance through a kind of 'magnificent hypocrisy' employed 'not to mislead but to embrace the possibilities inherent in the incorrigibly plural'. 'Snow' is a short lyric powerful beyond its small frame because it gives succinct expression to such a complex philosophical outlook. It is expounded at length in *Autumn Journal,* offsetting MacNeice's routine fatalism with an 'assertion of determined hope'. MacNeice's hopefulness combined the poet's conviction with that of his father, which Jon Stallworthy called 'the Bishop's integrity'.[18] The probity of the poet's father, John Frederick MacNeice, extended, as Louis's son Dan observed in 1987, to the performance of 'many courageous acts that probably would have got him lynched today'.[19] Louis absorbed and transmuted this courage, rejecting the core belief but retaining the practical component of his father's faith. Perhaps the single aspect of this practicality which carries most strongly across the years is an ability to communicate warmly and directly. MacNeice does so in a distinctive voice, one that is measured, amused and tolerant.

Anyone who has heard Luke Kelly declaim the opening stanza of 'Dublin',[20] a semi-finalist in RTÉ's 'poem for Ireland' contest, or stumbled across YouTube footage of a homeless man in Galway reciting the poem, will recognise that this voice could accommodate rhetorical flight and yearning sentiment within its sceptical purview. MacNeice's was a poetry built around towns that were not his, around 'ghosts that walk | And all that hide', and the 'bravado of talk' and 'days ... soft, | Soft enough to forget | The lesson better learnt'.[21] As this book shows, it is through a 'hard-headed recognition of pity gained through experience' that the balance is struck.

James Ward
Lecturer in English Literature
University of Ulster

NOTES

Quotes in the foreword without an accompanying citation are from this book.

1   Louis MacNeice, 'Carrick Revisited', pp.261–2 (p.261).
2   Louis MacNeice, 'Carrickfergus', pp.55–6 (p.55).
3   Louis MacNeice, 'Autobiography', pp.200–1 (p.200).
4   See Derek Mahon's 1972 poem of the same name in *A Rage for Order: Poetry of the Northern Ireland Troubles*, ed. Frank Ormsby (Belfast: Blackstaff, 1992), p.229.
5   Nick Laird, 'The Seal and the Cat', *Incorrigibly Plural: Louis MacNeice and His Legacy*, ed. Edna Longley and Fran Brearton (Manchester: Carcanet, 2012), pp.274–6 (p.275).
6   John Kerrigan, 'The Ticking Fear', rev. of *Louis MacNeice: Collected Poems*, ed. Peter McDonald (London: Faber, 2007), *Louis MacNeice: Selected Poems*, ed. Michael Longley (London: Faber, 2007), *I Crossed the Minch* by Louis MacNeice (London: Polygon, 2007) and *The Strings Are False: An Unfinished Autobiography* by Louis MacNeice, ed. E.R. Dodds (London: Faber, 2007), *London Review of Books* 30:3 (7 February 2008), pp.15–18.
7   Terence Brown, 'MacNeice and the Puritan Tradition', in *Louis MacNeice and His Influence*, ed. Kathleen Devine and Alan J. Peacock, Ulster Editions and Monographs 6 (Gerrards Cross: Colin Smythe, 1997), pp.20–33. Alan Gillis, '"Any Dark Saying": Louis MacNeice in the Nineteen Fifties', *Irish University Review*, 42:1 (2012), pp.105–23 (p.106).
8   Cyril Connolly claims to have invented the phrase after reading Stephen Spender's 'The Pylons', in *Poems* (London: Faber, 1933), pp.47–48. There is some dispute about Connolly's claim.
9   Louis MacNeice, *Autumn Journal*, III, p.105.
10 Louis MacNeice, 'Postscript', p.250. [Retitled 'When we were children' – from the opening words of the poem – for the first collected edition (London: Faber, 1948), when it was no longer the final poem, as it had been in *Springboard* (London: Faber, 1944)].
11 Louis MacNeice, 'A Comment', *New Verse*, 14 (April 1935), p.26.
12 Louis MacNeice, 'Snow', p.24.
13 Ibid.
14 Louis MacNeice, 'Alcohol', p.229–30 (p.229).
15 MacNeice, 'Postscript', p.250.

16   MacNeice, 'Carrick Revisited', pp.261–62 (p.262)

17   Louis MacNeice, 'Aubade for Infants', p.270.

18   Jon Stallworthy, *Louis MacNeice* (London: Faber, 1995), p.484.

19   Dan MacNeice, 'Memoirs', in *Incorrigibly Plural*, pp.25–41 (p.28).

20   'Dublin' is section one of 'The Coming of War (*Dublin, Cushendun, the West of Ireland, and back*)', pp.680–1.

21   MacNeice, 'The Coming of War', I 'Dublin', p.680–1.

CHAPTER 1

Louis MacNeice

On 24 January 1953, Jackie Kyle, captaining Ireland for the first time, opened the scoring with a dazzling solo run in the Five Nations match against France. It was the start of a successful day in front of a capacity crowd at Ravenhill Park in Belfast, Kyle's hometown. Among the 38,000 in attendance, two other Belfast natives watched with delight. One, a sculptor, still lived in Belfast; the other, a BBC radio dramatist and producer, was a London resident combining a business trip with the chance to watch the Irish take on France. The final score was 16–3 in Ireland's favour. Paul McWeeney took to verse in the *Sunday Independent* to celebrate 'our good fortune at Ravenhill yesterday':

> They seek him here, they seek him there,
> Those Frenchies seek him everywhere.
> That paragon of pace and guile,
> That damned elusive Jackie Kyle.[1]

Reflecting on the match, the émigré, who was better known as a poet than was the sports journalist McWeeney, turned to his friend and said, 'I'd give anything to be able to play like Jackie Kyle.' It wasn't long before the sculptor, George McCann, saw the recently graduated Queens University, Belfast, medical student Jackie Kyle and repeated those words of praise. Kyle's response was as quick as his on-field footwork, and he told McCann that he, in turn, would 'give anything to be able to write poetry like Louis MacNeice'.[2]

Louis MacNeice could be quiet and withdrawn, at times brusque and seemingly judgemental, but he had his joys, his delights, his passions and his pleasures. Rugby was one of them. Anthony Thwaite captured the two sides of MacNeice: 'Uncertain of your mood, after an hour | Of a shared office going slowly sour | With cigarettes and hangovers'

> I try the Twickenham ploy, the sort of war
> You relish, England – Ireland, worth an ode
> Better than J. C. Squire tried long ago.
> That does it. You prefer such stuff to bleak
> Intensities of bookishness, and speak
> With passion of who scored, and how, and know
> Each quiddity of form and style and skill.[3]

Geoffrey Grigson would remember MacNeice as 'our Pasternak … loyal to the Earth of the World',[4] a poet whose greatest strengths lay in the sensual and the immediate, who chose to celebrate the personal even as he hoped for improvement to society as a whole, who 'inscribed'

> With invisible legible letters
> That unrest of the soul
> Which you found
> So wryly appalling.[5]

'Mild and peaceful he was … or wanted to be … Romantic he was, if sceptical',[6] and there could be 'no doubting the degree of his delights, or the way so many poets have envied and turned against him on that score'.[7] He was a man and a poet who, when 'Death in his deep pothole caught' him, left behind 'no fake | Solution proffered to us all'.[8]

According to Richard Elman, MacNeice

> was a poet of wit and ingenuity, a parodist who spoke to be ironic and who seemed compelled to describe all experience obliquely, occasionally parodying himself, and usually avoiding direct iambic movement, or using it only to make a mockery of it … to stay alive [he] had to argue well. He was imitated; later he was even parodied; or he was attacked straight on; yet he survived and continued writing,

and was one of the few poets that I know of to have made a relatively successful use of accentual meters in English.[9]

When Seamus Heaney graduated in 1961 from Jackie Kyle's alma mater, one of the first books he bought was MacNeice's *Collected Poems 1925– 1948*, wherein 'I recognized his warm and clinkered spirit'.[10] Heaney's passport might have been 'green | No glass of ours was ever raised | To toast the Queen',[11] but MacNeice, whose passport was blue but on occasion also green, and whose father's public prayers always included an intersession for the king, and who for a while rented a home from the Crown Estate, 'did not allow the border to enter into his [literary] imaginings', and his 'sense of cultural diversity ... within the country never congealed into a red and green map'.[12] And so MacNeice was one of the five cornerstones of Heaney's 'quincunx' of Irish towers, represented in his case by the Norman castle at Carrickfergus. He was, Heaney suggested, 'faithful to his Ulster inheritance, his Irish affections and his English predilections'.[13]

When he was satirised, the attacks could be cheap and easy, as in Roy Campbell's lumping together of the 'MacSpaunday' poets in *Talking Bronco* – although it should be noted that even Campbell was apparently unsure of the appropriateness of conjoining MacNeice with Stephen Spender, W.H. Auden, and C. Day Lewis, and he occasionally prefers 'Spaunday' in the poem, dropping the Mac.[14] But at times the satire captures the 'clinkered spirit' Heaney recognised and reinforces the contagious nature of a poet who had been a classics professor.

Part of MacNeice's role as a lecturer had been 'Revealing the ageless to the briefly young | Explaining the dead to the living'.[15] He was a poet willing

> ... to pick at the seam of this discipline,
> Which presents the apotheosis as the norm,
> Which dresses the writers, the dramatists,
> The hypocrites, the philosophers and the lads
> Who drew right-angles in the sand with sticks,
> As the standard, the usual things
> Done in the usual way.[16]

MacNeice's 'personality declared itself along with ... events, gaining coherence as they lost it'.[17] His determination to preserve verse metres and structures others thought past their time was not stubbornness but a recognition that the past is present in the present. He undertook an entire volume in terza rima, fully aware, as Douglas Dunn put it, that

> The obsolete's
> Established as a form (like this), parodic
> Purloining a thirteenth-century beat,
>
> Dante's drum-kit, a metronomic tick,
> While those intent on being 'of the Age'
> Doodle devoutly in a Bolshevik
>
> Modernist manner's nervous prose.[18]

During a visit to the State University of New York at Albany in 1998, Paul Muldoon noted that MacNeice helped reassure subsequent Irish poets that the belief that 'art, poetry, must make something happen' was a belief worth holding, and that

> at some level [poetry] has to change the world, not necessarily in terms of mind-bendingly, extravagantly, huge ways … that would equal a cure for cancer or AIDS, or that would either bring peace to the world or topple governments. Not necessarily in any of those ways. But just in ways as simple as the fact that ideally one should … at some level, never to be able to stand at a bus stop again in exactly the same light, never to look in a culvert again in exactly the same light, never to think of what the open sea might mean in the same light.[19]

Changing the world was never a task MacNeice thought appropriate to himself, but he distrusted the order into which he had been born and in which he lived. He wanted not to take it apart but to enliven and enrich it with the human values of warmth, decency and integrity. His honesty in the face of his doubts remains startling even now: Medbh McGuckian 'cannot read "Prayer Before Birth" without being deeply frightened'.[20]

MacNeice himself was often deeply frightened of the chasm between the desired and the possible. Raised in a house where confidence in eternal salvation survived long periods tested by temporal trials, MacNeice found his voice in poems and dramas that, in the words of Frank Ormsby, 'offered

… ways of being simultaneously oblique and immediate'.[21] Ormsby's 'From the German' was inspired by *Autumn Journal* and its recognition of an 'inviolable presence' that only the human spirit can restore, 'some treacherous gift of innocence' MacNeice celebrated as the essence of the human condition.[22]

Like his contemporary fellow Ulster poet, John Hewitt, MacNeice subscribed to the lesson that the

> only hope now is to tame our tongues,
> trim them to the truth, for all within the place
> endure the same indignities and wrongs,
> the common fortune of our human race.[23]

MacNeice carried that lesson from out of Ireland and out of Ulster. Aloof and withdrawn though others might have found him, he did not pretend he was alone in his endeavours, and from his fellow Ulsterman once came the praise that 'Yr. defence of contemporary poets was an invaluable piece of work, especially in a cultural Sahara such as this'.[24]

Despite his classics training and his enormous breadth and depth of reading, MacNeice was too human to be 'of the character of myth',[25] but in London in 1953 working on the script for the documentary 'The Conquest of Everest'[26] he met John Berryman, who found after meeting him that his 'thoughts rushed onto a thousand screens | & Louis [was] the midwife of it'.[27] Not mythic but aware of all the myths, he 'never fixed on a single system of style – just as he never accepted the validity of a single system of thought or belief – so much the better'.[28]

MacNeice was also aware that one of the incongruities of being an Irish Protestant by culture if not faith is that 'you're Irish when you're in Britain, but you're not Irish when you're in Ireland. You're a bad fit everywhere'.[29] MacNeice acknowledged and so celebrated the incongruous. His most anthologised poem, 'Snow', resonates not only for its technically accomplished yet deftly handled form but also for its praise of the propinquity of the unexpectedly specific. Jean Bleakney identifies two lines from the poem as

> among my favourite and most quotable lines from any poet. There is so much colour and energy and music in his work. His voice seems so intelligent and questioning. I love the recurrence of the word

'between'; from an early poem 'Spring Sunshine' (1929) which opens, 'In a between world, a bottom world of amber' to one of his last 'Coda' (1962), 'There are moments caught between heartbeats | When maybe we know each other better'. I've learnt a lot about poetry, and life, from MacNeice.[30]

'Snow' has become such a touchstone poets can call upon it as a common cultural reference, even those such as Ciaran Carson who 'haven't read that much MacNeice'.[31] The 'bay window' of the opening line of Carson's 'Belfast Confetti', the ping-pong ball coming to an 'incorrigible' stop, the 'snow and roses just behind | The bullet-proof glass' in the bank, the 'soundlessly collateral' auction bidding for a couch from the 1930s and memories of the day in Carson's childhood when 'Roses are brought in, and suddenly, white confetti seethes against the window' all point directly to MacNeice's poem.[32]

MacNeice died of pneumonia just shy of his 56th birthday in a London hospital, where he had quizzed the doctors gathered around his bed with the question, 'Am I supposed to be dying?'[33] A month earlier he had reportedly told Robert Lowell 'It's better | to die at fifty than lose my pleasure in terror'.[34]

In Ireland, he might well have been about to enjoy a resurgence of reputation. He was 'the only [Ulster] poet whose work we would see reviewed in the newspapers', even if he was maligned by the idea that 'he only came to Belfast for rugby matches!'[35] That after 1954 those matches were played exclusively in Dublin only serves to underscore MacNeice's disregard for the border. Just a year after his death, three then unpublished poets drove to Carrowdore churchyard in County Down, where MacNeice was buried beside his mother. Michael Longley, Seamus Heaney and Derek Mahon

> dawdled between the graves … each contemplating an elegy … We felt bereaved of a father-figure whom we had only recently been getting to know. (Mahon was the only one of us who had met him personally). The return of his ashes to Ireland did feel like some kind repatriation. When the three of us were next together Mahon took from his pocket 'In Carrowdore Churchyard' and read it aloud. Heaney started to recite his poem, then crumpled it up. I wisely decided then and there not to make the attempt. Mahon had

produced the definitive elegy.[36]

It was an elegy that opened Mahon's first collection, *Twelve Poems*, and also his *Selected Poems*, a significant testament to the value Mahon places on MacNeice's importance. It is a poem that subtly draws out the strength implicit in MacNeice's careful attention to the subjunctive and the conditional as the means through which we can assert our identity and our integrity in the face of the pity that fills a world where what should be can only be intimated:

This, you implied, is how we ought to live –

The ironical, loving crush of roses against snow,
Each fragile, solving ambiguity.[37]

NOTES

1   A. P[aul] McWeeney, 'Kyle's Genius the Highlight of Great Win over France', *Sunday Independent*, 25 January 1953, p.10.
2   Mercy McCann [wife of George] to Jon Stallworthy; qtd in Jon Stallworthy, *Louis MacNeice* (London: Faber, 1995) p.395.
3   Anthony Thwaite, 'For Louis MacNeice', *Times Literary Supplement*, 3706 (16 March 1973), p.292; repr. in Terence Brown and Alec Reid (eds), *Time Was Away: The World of Louis MacNeice* (Dublin: Dolmen, 1974), pp.111–12 (p.111). [The Squire reference is to J[ohn] C[ollings] Squire, *The Rugger Match* (London: privately published, 1922).]
4   Geoffrey Grigson, 'Louis MacNeice', in *Recollections: Mainly of Writers and Artists* (London: Chatto and Windus, 1984), pp.72–6 (p.72).
5   Geoffrey Grigson, 'Louis MacNeice', *A Skull in Salop and Other Poems* (Chester Springs, PA: Dufour, 1969), pp.11–12 (p.12).
6   Grigson, *Recollections*, p.75.
7   Ibid., p.73.
8   Geoffrey Grigson, 'After Reading an Autobiography', *A Skull in Salop*, pp.44–5 (p.45).
9   Richard Elman, 'The Legacy of Louis MacNeice', *The New Republic*, 149:17 (26 October 1963), p.19.
10 Louis MacNeice, *Collected Poems, 1925–1948* (London: Faber, 1949); Seamus Heaney, 'The Placeless Heaven: Another Look at Kavanagh', in *The Government of the Tongue: Selected Prose, 1978–1987* (London: Faber, 1988), pp.3–14 (p.8).
11 Seamus Heaney, 'Open Letter', Field Day Pamphlet 2 (Derry: Field Day, 1983), p.9.
12 Seamus Heaney, 'Frontiers of Writing', in *The Redress of Poetry* (London: Faber, 1995), pp.186–203 (pp.198–9).
13 Ibid., p.200.

14   Roy Campbell, *Talking Bronco* (London: Faber, 1946).

15   John Clarke, 'What I Did in the Holidays', *The Even More Complete Book of Australian Verse* (Melbourne: Text, 2003), pp.75–6 (p.75).

16   Ibid., p.76.

17   Clive James, 'Preface' to 'Poem of the Year', *The Book of My Enemy: Collected Verse 1958–2003* (London: Picador, 2003), pp.247–9 (p.247).

18   Douglas Dunn, 'Disenchantments', in *Dante's Drum-Kit* (London: Faber, 1993), pp.31–46 (pp.37–38).

19   'The Invention of the I: A Conversation with Paul Muldoon' [Paul Muldoon in conversation with Stan Rubin and Earl Ingersoll, 4 April 1996], *Michigan Quarterly Review*, 37:1 (winter 1996), pp.67–73. <http://hdl.handle.net/2027/spo.act2080.0037.106>accessed 20 April 2015.

20   John Brown (ed.), *In the Chair: Interviews with Poets from the North of Ireland* (Cliffs of Moher: Salmon, 2002), pp.176–7.

21   Brown, *In the Chair*, p.133.

22   Frank Ormsby, 'From the German', *A Northern Spring* (Dublin: Gallery, 1986), p.36.

23   John Hewitt, 'A Little People', *The Collected Poems of John Hewitt*, ed. Frank Ormsby (Belfast: Blackstaff, 1991), pp.539–41 (p.540).

24   John Hewitt to Louis MacNeice, 12 July 1939, p.350n.

25   John Berryman, 'Dream Song 267', *The Dream Songs* (New York, NY: Farrar, Strauss and Giroux, 1969), p.286.

26   'The Conquest of Everest', dir. George Lowe, British Lion Film, 1953.

27   Berryman, 'Dream Song 267', p.286.

28   Nick Laird, 'Chianti in Khartoum', rev. of *Letters of Louis MacNeice*, (ed.) Jonathan Allison (London: Faber, 2010), *London Review of Books*, 33:5 (March 2011), pp.31–3 (p.31).

29   Nicholas Wroe, 'Nick Laird: A Life in Writing', *The Guardian*, 4 January 2013.<http://www.theguardian.com/books/2013/jan/04/nick-laird-life-in-writing> accessed 25 April 2015.

30   Brown, *In the Chair*, p.221.

31   Ibid., p.149

32   Ciaran Carson, 'Belfast Confetti', *Belfast Confetti* (Oldcastle: Gallery, 1989), p.67.

33   Stallworthy, *MacNeice*, p.477.

34   Robert Lowell, 'The House-Party (For Louis MacNeice 1907–1963)', *Notebook* (London: Faber, 1970), p.202.

35   Brown, *In the Chair*, p.89.

36   Michael Longley, 'Introduction', *Louis MacNeice: Poems Selected by Michael Longley* (London: Faber, 2001), pp.vii–xii (p.xi).

37   Derek Mahon, 'In Carrowdore Graveyard (at the Grave of Louis MacNeice)', *Selected Poems* (Oldcastle: Gallery, 2000), p.11.

CHAPTER 2

Historical and Cultural Contexts

Frederick Louis MacNeice was born in Belfast 'between the mountain and the gantries'.[1] He would spend much of his life 'between' things. In part, he would identify this sense of separation and a reluctance he saw in himself to join groups as a familial heritage. In part, his sense of being between possible end points, between the mountains and the gantries, was a self-conscious response to alternatives that were all problematic. In part, his distance was imposed on him by his birth in a country that would soon be divided. He would find his voice just as the culture from which he drew part of his experience came to learn that it 'had been spiritually hyphenated without knowing it', as Stephen Gwynn said, reflecting on post-1922 Ireland and the discovery that 'the new nationalism prefer[red] to describe me and the like of as Anglo-Irish'.[2]

In the midst of so much cultural and political change, perhaps it was not surprising that when he went up to Oxford the freshly minted undergraduate dropped Frederick from all but legal documents and was henceforward known as Louis. Such re-identification, however, was already a familial trait. His father used his first name, John, only on formal occasions, and a cousin, Donor, the last of various scions of the family to serve as an Anglican priest, dropped his first name, Alan, from all but the Irish passport which accompanied him to work in Hawaii and Cambodia. Donor's 'father was John Herbert Macneice, but until he died I never knew he had the name John'.[3] Louis's sister, Caroline, went by Elizabeth from early in her life and throughout her medical career. The MacNeices would seem to have been a family intent on self-creation.

Louis MacNeice was born on 12 September 1907, the last of the three children of Elizabeth Margaret, 'Lily', MacNeice, née Cleshan, and John Frederick MacNeice, then rector of Holy Trinity Church, situated just opposite Clifton House on what is now Clifton Street.[4] John had been born on the Isle of Omey, County Galway, the son of a Society of Irish Church Missions school teacher, and Lily in Ballymacrony, County Galway, where she would later be an Irish Church Missions teacher. John graduated from Trinity College, Dublin, in 1895 and was ordained in 1897. The couple married after he accepted the position of rector of St Clement's, in Ballymacarett, East Belfast, in 1902. The next year, he returned to Holy Trinity, where he had been a curate, and Elizabeth was born on 24 April. The family then moved to 1 Brookhill Avenue where William Lindsay was born on 31 March 1905.[5] Louis was born two and a half years later in the same house.

The house in Belfast was in a Church of Ireland parish with a congregation distinctly working class and very much involved with the Orange Order. The rector was part of that community. This ability to connect with solidly working-class Unionist Church of Ireland congregants despite being a Dublin-educated Connemara native and a lifetime teetotaller reveals most of what needs to be known about the effectiveness of the cleric's approach to his calling. Like his father, the rector's son never made the easy mistake of assuming that work is inherently dignified. Dignity, both knew, is an expression of human will, not of the economic value of the toil, and it often comes at great cost. Many years later, Louis would ask of a woman dying in poverty who had kept her household and family together:

> given her grim
> Good humour – her daily tonic against despair,
> Given her wakeful nights trying to balance the budget
> And given her ignorance of her own frailty,
> What other end was coming?[6]

Yet even if her family did 'not see that the only cable was broken | That held them together, self-respecting and sane',[7] her self-respect and self-consciousness defined a life worth living.

The first great upheaval that would help substantiate Louis's permanent sense of not quite belonging anywhere came just more than a year after his birth. His father was offered the living as rector of St Nicholas, Carrickfergus, County Antrim, after much heated debate within the parish. He was instituted in the parish church on 25 November 1908. At least initially, he was an unpopular choice.[8] The family moved to rented accommodation in Carrickfergus until the rectory became available and awaited the usual roll call of visitors. Lily set out the biscuits and cakes each day for a week and each day for a week, so the story goes, no one called.[9]

The new congregation was very different to those the rector had known before. St Nicholas had for centuries been the church of the Chichester family, the marquesses of Donegall, and it retained a significant atmosphere of rural privilege. The Church of Ireland community was a minority within the broader Protestant population and more obviously 'establishment' than had been the congregations at either St Clement's or Holy Trinity.

Covenant Day 1912 was a turning point in the rector's career. It marked a public shift from practices that embodied relatively traditional if devout Church of Ireland practices to one that would see him henceforward conduct his life based on a far more outward understanding of the word 'Christianity', drawing for inspiration on the Oxford Movement and, later, on the ideas of his contemporary William Temple, who would end his career as the Archbishop of Canterbury.

On Saturday 28 September 1912 flags and bunting dominated the streets of Carrickfergus as the Unionist procession made its way through the town centre until one group headed for services at St Nicholas and others to a united service at the Joymount Presbyterian church. MacNeice stood in his pulpit and told the assembled congregation that the Covenant was 'a call to arms' and the 'Church of Christ ... cannot sound that call. The Church as a Church, fighting for her own life, must fight under Christ's banner and in Christ's way'.[10] It was a 'grand sermon the rector gave us', reported Tommy Robinson, the butcher, 'but he spoilt it all at the end by telling us he wasn't going to sign the Covenant.'[11]

After the services, the congregations gathered at the courthouse, which is now the town hall, to sign the Covenant. MacNeice, John Minford, the minister of the Joymount Presbyterian church, and the ministers of the First Presbyterian church, of the Methodist chapel and of the Congregational church all refused to sign. This stance taken by so many Protestant clerics in a single community was unique to Carrickfergus. The *Ulster Guardian* noted that 'Men who can face the angry looks of friends as a matter of principle will never run away from the foe … and no one who knows the history of Carrickfergus and of St Nicholas's parish for the past few years will fail to estimate correctly the amount of pluck that was behind the simple confession of the rector on Saturday last.'[12] For the young Louis, Covenant Day could only have helped reinforce his emerging sense that there was one world within the garden of the rectory and another outside it.

The rector would remain a cleric who lived by the certainties of his convictions. One of the last surviving priests to be ordained by MacNeice remembered that he

> was generally hostile to St George's [in Belfast] both to its attitude and indeed existence. He was evidently very critical of the way St George's depended on pew rents for its support … St George's changed its policy and provided free pews in the back for all comers but the bishop gave the parish no credit for this in what he wrote in [*The Church of Ireland in Belfast*] … Willy Kirkpatrick, a deeply spiritual man in the High Church tradition … who … for many years and with his sister provided a kind of on-going presence of prayer and earthly spirituality would always shake his head sadly when [MacNeice] was due to visit.[13]

In the midst of a broader public act, something else might well have begun to occur to the young boy, as it was surely affecting his father: 'Ireland' was a concept whose meaning shifted across geography and economics and religion. Louis would not have to grapple directly with the political implications of Irish partition, but at the outbreak of hostilities in 1914 'it was some time before I could make out whether it was the English or the Germans who were the enemy.'[14] Youthful confusion about the enemy might well have been more than the simple interest of a young schoolboy in getting noticed, for even within the rector's household there was less than whole-hearted support for his position. Margaret MacCready, the daughter of an Antrim farmer and 'mother's helper' in the rectory, was heard reporting that her 'father … would as soon have the Kaiser as King George any day. The Kaiser is a good Protestant.'[15]

Louis would later claim his father 'fixed | His pulpit out of the reach of party slogans,'[16] and the rector was certainly influenced by Sterling

Berry, Bishop of Killaloe, who used the April 1915 edition of the *Irish Church Quarterly* to attack comments made in an earlier issue by Charles Frederick D'Arcy, then Bishop of Down and Connor and Dromore, which both justified war with Germany and could be read as supporting armed resistance to Home Rule without partition. Berry found no 'loophole' in the Sermon on the Mount, and while he agreed that Britain's treaty obligations required it to defend Belgium he argued that the need to invoke these obligations was the 'result of the unChristian principles that had dominated the life of western Christendom and of which both Church and nation need to repent'.[17] Berry's view – that 'if a nation is compelled to choose between two courses, both of them evil, it usually results from wrong or folly of which the nation was guilty before the choice had to be made'[18] – was one that John Frederick MacNeice increasingly came to share.

Louis would seem later to have taken his father's stance to have been that of a Home Ruler, as did many of the rector's congregants, but this was to mistake the situation. The rector never renounced his identification of himself as a Unionist. But his Unionism, like Berry's, was of the politically untenable brand strongest among Church of Ireland adherents in the southern and western counties. If the elder MacNeice was hardly alone in thinking that the First World War and the Anglo-Irish Treaty had changed 'practically everything in the political order',[19] his reaction was distinctive. The appropriate response to political disruption, he said, was to look beyond, rather than deny, change and to speak for, and represent, a Christian ideal, and so, 'a true patriot if he had vision as well as zeal, even though he counted it an injustice that Ireland which was geographically "one" should be politically "two", [would] rather wait five years, ten years, any number of years than attempt to lay the foundations of Irish unity in Irish blood'.[20]

Even as events in Carrickfergus offered the young Louis a confusing lesson in politics, life within the rectory turned from difficult to painful. Lily had been ill for some time, mainly with a 'gynaecological complaint' that would seem to have begun in 1910 but which was not diagnosed until later and which had various intermittent physical manifestations.[21] Her illness was complicated by increasingly severe and lengthy depression. Early in 1913, a visit to a gynaecologist in Belfast brought the news that a hysterectomy was necessary. Elizabeth would later record that her mother believed at least part of the cause of the uterine fibroid which required the operation had been Louis's difficult birth.[22] This would not have been so, but Louis shared his mother's conviction: 'The day I was born | I suppose that that same hour was full of her screams.'[23]

The surgery was a success, but Lily's post-operative depression was deeper than ever, and she 'change[d] almost overnight from a mother who had always been the mainstay of the household ... the very essence of stability – into someone who was deeply unhappy and no longer able to make decisions.'[24] By the end of August, her husband had decided Lily would best be provided for in a Dublin nursing home run by a friend. Elizabeth's and Louis's last sight of their mother was of her getting into one of the few cars in Carrickfergus and she and her husband being driven to the station for the Belfast train and, hence, a connection to Dublin. MacNeice's sixth birthday was the month after Lily left Carrickfergus. It was a difficult time. He received a birthday present from his mother, but none of the children would get to visit her before her death from tuberculosis in December 1914.

While the departure and then death of their mother was painful for the children, it was excruciating for her husband. His copy of Alfred Plummer's *Exegetical Commentary on the Gospel According to S. Matthew* is, as was typical of his books, full of marginalia and underlining. The section on Matt. XIX 3-12 ('The Question of Divorce') is particularly heavily marked, in plain pencil, red pencil and blue pencil, indicating he read it on at least three occasions. One section is revisited every time: 'Christ's argument for the indissoluble character of the original institution of marriage is that at the Creation God made one man and one woman for each other ... He created a relation between man and wife more intimate and binding than even that between parent and child.'[25] This latter sentence is underlined in red and marked in the margin with a blue vertical line. Perhaps the rector drew some comfort from the fact that in the next section, 'The Blessing of the Little Children', Plummer stressed that the sequence of discussion in Matthew of marriage, the little children and wealth in that order makes perfect sense.[26] You can almost feel the relief MacNeice felt as he wrote in pencil below the text the list 'Marriage | Little Children | Wealth.'[27] Whatever the moods of the house, the children, though they did not know it, must have been a great comfort to their father.

Louis and Elizabeth began spending much of their time avoiding the moods of the house by playing a complex game probably initiated by Elizabeth when she invented 'the Great Queen (or Mrs) Mac Niss.'[28]

In his unfinished autobiography, *The Strings Are False*, MacNeice prefers the spelling 'MacNisque'; either way, 'Louis's imagination soon took over and a whole host of invisible people came to live in the trees and bushes and sheds … We spent hours conversing with them and even asked their advice.'[29] At the same time, the children were somewhat isolated from their peers in Carrickfergus, keeping to themselves in the rectory garden or being escorted on buggy drives in the vicinity. Their father's observation of the Sabbath meant they were forbidden from playing on Sundays, and MacNeice recalled 'the great gulf between myself and the barefoot boys in the streets', and when he 'passed the men who stood most of the day, spitting, at the corners, I imagined they were spitting at me'.[30]

After Lily's departure, the house remained very much 'hers'[31] and the mood in the rectory became 'very sad'.[32] Perhaps recollecting this period, MacNeice would have the heroine of his one published novel, *Roundabout Way*, reflect on her father's remote sternness:

> 'Men go queer without wives,' Janet thought … 'if mother hadn't died he'd never have got like this … He likes one a lot and then he goes and mucks one up …'
>
> 'If mother hadn't died,' she thought, and her mind strolled away, into the parks of memory – parks with no placards, no keep-off-the-grasses … She held a balloon on a string (always terrified of it popping), flaunting and bobbing on the end of a string. And at mid-day when the others had lunch, she looked forward to her soup-plate of pure cream and sugar – everyone, Dads especially, had been horrified when she started this habit, but her mother had said it was all to the good if she liked it.[33]

Then, in 1917, the rector married Georgina Beatrice, 'Bea', Greer, a parishioner in her forties and a member of the wealthiest family in the area, whose home was Seapark – now the district headquarters of the Police Service of Northern Ireland – but who also spent considerable time in a Regent's Park mansion, and it was in London that the marriage took place. It was to be a long and happy union and introduced the MacNeices to a social world to which they had had relatively little exposure. The 'gentry [whom] I did not like … were patronising and snobbish and, it seemed to me, hostile', Louis wrote about his new family's circle, although he admitted that 'the hostility I almost certainly exaggerated'.[34] More than forty years later, he recalled what would have been one of his first visits to the Greer house:

> And these were the joys of that house: a tower with a telescope;
> Two great faded globes, one of the earth, one of the stars;
> A stuffed black dog in the hall; a walled garden with bees;
> A rabbit warren; a rockery; a vine under glass; the sea.[35]

Elizabeth remembered that 'no children could have had a kinder or more generous stepmother, and Louis in particular became very fond of her', but she also 'introduced a Puritan spirit into the house … and this led to restrictions which my father alone would not have imposed'.[36] Louis found her arrival 'brought so much comfort and benevolence … I dropped my resolution to obstruct'.[37] Nonetheless, many years later he would recall 'my step-mother bursting into tears … because she thought Elizabeth & I only owed allegiance to my father'.[38] But Bea also chastised Elizabeth and Louis 'because, she said, we always left the room whenever my father entered it. Which, I think, was true!'[39]

Not long after their father's marriage, Elizabeth and Louis went to school in England. This in itself marked a major change in MacNeice family tradition, whose children had until then been schooled in Church of Ireland schools. Additionally, Bea was in favour of an English education so that both children might lose their Ulster accents. This was not entirely successful, as recordings of Louis reading his poetry demonstrate.

MacNeice attended Sherborne College's preparatory school and then Marlborough. The prep headmaster was Littleton Powys, 'Who taught me the names of butterflies and the tricks || Of Latin elegiacs' and 'so brought | Us children to our senses. Which were five'.[40] MacNeice's father had instructed his son in Latin, but Louis had found the effort unrewarding and difficult. The son of a schoolteacher, however, retained at least some of his talent and, years later, Louis's own son, Dan, would remember that his grandfather 'taught me to read in about three weeks, when I was about five – a meteoric period which now astonishes me … His pedagogic talents must have been remarkable and I'm sure he would have made an excellent teacher had he chosen to follow in his father's profession.'[41] Whatever the case, Louis quickly demonstrated a facility with the nuances of language: Asked on a train in spring 1919 on his way back to school what he thought of Sir Edward Carson, Louis, 'remembering my father and Home Rule …

said I thought Carson was a pity.'[42] The choice of that last word reveals a budding classicist's understanding of the root word 'pietas' informed also by a deeply moral Christian upbringing, better encapsulating the situation than did many long essays.

At home, as well as being a dedicated player of the 'Mac Niss' game Louis had been a keen reader of fairy tales, and at Sherborne he read Malory's *Morte d'Arthur*, 'sitting in a windowseat and reading with such concentration that my hair stuck to the paint of the woodwork … I revelled in the reiteration of incident; to go from joust to joust and count how many knights [were] unseated was as exciting as reading the County Cricket batting averages'.[43] His 'chief verse-reading for two years' was Palgrave's *Golden Treasury*, and, at least as MacNeice recalled it later, 'during this period I underwent a coarsening of taste and a growing preference for what Yeats called those "crude, violent rhythms as of a man running"'.[44] He read John Keats's 'Endymion' and 'Hyperion', most of John Milton's *Paradise Lost* and Edmund Spenser's *The Faerie Queene*. Keats was MacNeice's epitome of the ideal poet: 'I wanted "La Belle Dame Sans Merci". And self-pity had become an important factor. Keats was very sorry for himself. It had always been easy and pleasant to be sorry for oneself; now we knew that it was also a poetic occupation.'[45] In time, MacNeice would confront the distinction between indulgent self-pity and the hard-headed recognition of pity gained through experience: the difference between bathos and pathos. At times, others would accuse him of failing to recognise that distinction.

Fairy tales and allegories offered MacNeice a secular touchstone for his father's example of a Christian spiritual journey that gave purpose to life. At university, he

would feel rather hypocritical [in denying my father's faith], for, greatly though he now exasperated me, I would remember how my father would come in to breakfast on Easter Day beaming as though he had just received a legacy; and I realised that his life, though not by any stretch of imagination a life for me, was more all of a piece, more purposeful, more satisfactory to himself and perhaps to others than the lives of most people I knew.[46]

Louis looked to different symbols than his father, but he was no less cognisant of the importance of a life 'all of a piece'. Bea had introduced the family to books about missionaries and he had thought then of being one himself: 'in the end I should be martyred and clergymen would use me in sermons for a noble example'.[47] Quests were ennobling, in the finest sense of the word, a way of making meaning of a life – 'Put out to sea, ignoble comrades, | Whose record shall be noble yet'[48] – a way of asserting one's own identity and integrity. But a quest came, too, with the risk of becoming an end in itself and the wrong quest for the wrong reason was the most fatal choice of all. Ultimately, it was not the quest itself that ennobled but the generosity with which it was undertaken.

Louis MacNeice was 'a man who lost things: a mother when he was five, a wife and then a son, then his connection to another wife'.[49] In 1922, when he was 15, he had also lost a country, but in losing a politically defined Ireland he gained a place that already had mythic qualities imbued by stories from childhood of

> 'The West of Ireland', a phrase which still stirs me, if not like a trumpet, like a fiddle half heard through a cattle fair ... The very name Connemara seemed too rich for an ordinary place. It appeared to be a country of windswept open spaces and mountains blazing with whims and seas that were never quiet, and drowned palaces beneath them, and seals and eagles and turf smoke and cottagers who were always laughing and who gave you milk when you asked for a glass of water. And the people's voices were different there, soft and rich like my father's.[50]

He had been

> brought up in a very prosaic context on the northern shore of Belfast Lough ... but this did not undermine my belief that these [wild or fantastic] qualities were typical of a nation to which I was extremely proud to belong. I could always ignore the evidence around me on the ground that the real Irish lived in the South ... Being then autochthonous Irish and with a father who was at that time a Home Ruler I at an early age thought it was my religious duty to be a rebel and that the best of all terms of reproach was the word 'English'.[51]

'We are all homeless sometimes, homesick sometimes',[52] but homesickness is a difficult attribute for one who has no clear sense of home. Whatever his sympathies, Derek Mahon pointed out, MacNeice 'didn't, by class or religious background, "belong to the people". How then, not sharing the general constraints, could he free himself from them?'[53]

Perhaps inevitably, the answer MacNeice shaped had something to do with W.B. Yeats, himself 'a federation' but also a 'malingerer in fairyland'.[54] Yeats had anticipated events in Ireland by 'founding a one-man sect, remaking Ireland in a manner that still allowed him a role'.[55] MacNeice identified various failings to Yeats's stratagem, and he also recognised that only Yeats could have hoped to pull off the trick in the first place, but he thought there might be another federation to which he could belong, one identified, in an ironic twist of fate, by an Ulster dramatist of the generation before MacNeice, St John Greer Ervine, born in the rector's old parish of Ballymacarret in 1883. Ervine's 1923 *The Lady of Belmont* revisits Shylock, who announces at play's end that 'we cannot go back. We must go on and mingle with the world and lose ourselves in other men. I know that outward things pass and have no duration. There is nothing left but the goodness which a man performs.'[56]

Ervine's initial advocacy of an Ireland where 'Protestants and Catholics, Orangemen and Ancient Hibernians put their hands together and the four beautiful fields of Cathleen niHoulihan become one pasture'[57] gave way to a 'reactionary unionism and anti-southern hatred [that] became more pronounced as he aged and eclipsed his more subtle characteristics'.[58] It was this latter attitude MacNeice would recognise when he left to

> St John Ervine, ornament of the nation,
> His Ulster accent and les neiges d'antan
> And a little, if possible, accurate information.[59]

This poetic attack hinted at a side of MacNeice 'fierce … in words, in occasional controversy when his values were assailed, as … St John Ervine, who fancied himself as a superior and scornful controversialist, once learnt when battered by Louis in an exchange of letters in the *Observer*.'[60]

But the younger Belfast-born writer had a similar response to Ervine's Shylock when he looked to the 'Common Man', who 'is neither a pattern of virtue nor a potential world-saviour. But he has those virtues which, as Aristotle would say, are proper to him and he can, it seems, on occasions save himself.'[61]

NOTES

References to the poems of Louis MacNeice are as they appear in Peter McDonald (ed.), *Collected Poems* (London: Faber, 2007), except as noted.

1   Louis MacNeice, 'Carrickfergus', pp.55–6.

2   Stephen Gwynn, *Experiences of a Literary Man* (London: Butterworth, 1926), p.11. Incidentally, Gwynn wrote *Masters of English Literature* (London: Macmillan, 1904) which MacNeice had as a text book while at Marlborough. For more on Gwynn and the Ireland MacNeice never quite knew, see Colin Reid, *The Lost Ireland of Stephen Gwynn: Irish Constitutional Nationalism and Cultural Politics, 1864–1950* (Manchester: Manchester University Press, 2011).

3   Personal correspondence, 20 December 2004. Quite when the upper case 'N' made it into Louis's side of the family is not clear, but it was his father who added the 'a' to MacNeice. As late as 1911 he signed his copy of *An Exegetical Commentary of the Gospel According to S. Matthew* by Alfred Plummer (London: Elliot Stock, 1910) 'Frederick McNeice | Carrickfergus 1911'. At some stage, the letter 'a' was added in pencil. The Plummer volume is in my possession.

4   The current Holy Trinity was built on a different location after the Second World War, the church MacNeice served having been destroyed in the Belfast Blitz on the night of 15 April 1941. MacNeice was at the time Bishop of Down and Connor and Dromore and, hence, had episcopal oversight of the church. He would die the next year, before rebuilding plans had been made.

5   William had Down's syndrome and will make almost no further appearance in this book, which does a disservice to his family, who refused to accept the standard practice of the time and cared for him at home as much as possible, sending him to residential care only when it seemed unavoidable. After his stepmother died in 1956, he lived in England with his sister and died in 1968 at the then quite remarkable age of 63.

6   Louis MacNeice, 'The Kingdom', III, pp.241–9 (p.243–4).

7   Ibid., p.244.

8   For a full account of MacNeice's arrival at Carrickfergus and his work there to reconcile the various factions within the congregation, see David Fitzpatrick, *'Solitary and Wild': Frederick MacNeice and the Salvation of Ireland* (Dublin: Lilliput, 2012), chapter 6, 'Diplomat: Carrickfergus, 1908–1912', especially pp.94–8.

9   A less dramatic version of this story can be found in Jon Stallworthy, *Louis MacNeice* (London: Faber, 1995), p.21.

10 John Frederick MacNeice, *Carrickfergus and its Contacts: Some Chapters in the History of Ulster* (London: Simpkin, Marshall; Belfast: Erskine Mayne, 1928), pp.72–3.

11 Elizabeth Nicholson, 'Trees Were Green', in Terence Brown and Alec Reid (eds), *Time Was Away: The World of Louis MacNeice* (Dublin: Dolmen, 1974), pp.11–20 (p.15).

12 'A Brave Act', (second leader), *Ulster Guardian*, 5 October 1912; qtd in William T. McKinnon, 'The Rector's Son', *The Honest Ulsterman*, 73 (September 1983), pp.34–54 (pp.43-4).

13 J.R.B. ['Dick'] McDonald. Personal correspondence, 20 May 2001. When MacNeice's book appeared, St George's was still largely a pew-rent church, a state of affairs MacNeice

called a 'handicap' and a 'reproach'. John Frederick MacNeice, *The Church of Ireland in Belfast* (Belfast: Mullan, 1931), p.19.

14 Louis MacNeice, *The Poetry of W.B. Yeats* (Oxford: Oxford University Press, 1941; repr. London: Faber, 1967), p.52.

15 Qtd in Stallworthy, *MacNeice*, p.41.

16 W.H. Auden and Louis MacNeice, 'Auden and MacNeice: Their Last Will and Testament', in *Letters from Iceland* (London: Faber, 1937), pp.236–58 (p.238).

17 Andrew Scholes, *The Church of Ireland and the Third Home Rule Bill* (Dublin: Irish Academic Press, 2010), Scholes is lightly paraphrasing William Temple's account of the rationale behind a series of 'Papers for War Time', see, William Temple, *Church and Nation, the Bishop Paddock Lectures for 1914–15, Delivered at the General Theological Seminary, New York* (London: Macmillan 1915), p.ix. At the time, Temple was Chaplain to His Majesty the King.

18 Sterling Berry, 'The Ethics of War: A Reply', *Irish Church Quarterly*, 8:30 (April 1915), pp.102–11 (p.103).

19 John Frederick MacNeice, 'For Peace with Honour between North and South. An Address to Orangemen at a Special Service in the Parish Church, Carrickfergus, on Sunday 9th July 1922, Dedicated to Lady Frederick Cavendish' ([Carrickfergus: Bell, 1922]), pp.1–2. For the Church of Ireland and its bishops's responses to events at this time see, Scholes, *The Church of Ireland*.

20 MacNeice, 'Peace with Honour', p.3.

21 Louis MacNeice, *The Strings Are False: An Unfinished Autobiography*, ed. E.R. Dodds (London: Faber, 1965), pp.42–3n [note by Elizabeth Nicholson].

22 Nicholson, 'Trees Were Green', p.16.

23 Louis MacNeice, 'Eclogue Between the Motherless', pp.82–87 (p.84).

24 MacNeice, *Strings*, p.43n [note by Elizabeth Nicholson].

25 Plummer, *Exegetical Commentary*, p.261.

26 Ibid., pp.262–3.

27 Ibid., p.262.

28 Nicholson, 'Trees Were Green', p.19.

29 Ibid.

30 Louis MacNeice, 'Recantation', *The Honest Ulsterman*, 73 (September 1983), pp.4–9 (p.5).

31 Nicholson, 'Trees Were Green', p.19.

32 Ibid., p.17.

33 Louis Malone [Louis MacNeice], *Roundabout Way* (London: Putnam's, 1932); repr. as *'Roundabout Way' by Louis MacNeice* (London: Capuchin Classics, 2012), p.41.

34 MacNeice, 'Recantation', p.5.

35 Louis MacNeice, 'Soap Suds', p.577.

36 Nicholson, 'Trees Were Green', p.19.

37 MacNeice, *Strings*, p.61.

38 Louis MacNeice to Daniel MacNeice, 30 August 1952, p.552.

39 Ibid.

40 Louis MacNeice, *Autumn Sequel*, XXII, p.472.

41 Dan MacNeice, 'Rebecca', *Carrickfergus & District Historical Journal*, 7 (1993), p.51.

42 MacNeice, *Strings*, p.71.

43 Ibid., p.77.

44 Louis MacNeice, *Modern Poetry: A Personal Essay* (London: Oxford University Press, 1938), p.41.

45 Ibid., p.46.

46 Louis MacNeice, 'Landscapes of Childhood and Youth', in *Strings*, pp.216–38 (p.233).

47 MacNeice, *Strings*, p.61.

48 Louis MacNeice, 'Thalassa', p.783.

49 Kevin Andrews, 'Time and the Will Lie Sidestepped: Athens, the Interval', in *Time Was Away*, pp.103–10 (p.109).

50 Louis MacNeice, 'Landscapes', pp.216–17.

51 Louis MacNeice, *I Crossed the Minch* (London: Longmans, Green, 1938; repr. Edinburgh: Polygon, 2007), pp.29–30.

52 Louis MacNeice, 'Day of Returning', pp.355–6 (p.356).

53 Derek Mahon, 'MacNeice in England and Ireland', in *Time Was Away*, pp.113–22 (p.117).

54 MacNeice, *Modern Poetry*, pp.80–81.

55 Edna Longley, 'Louis MacNeice: The Walls are Flowing', in Gerald Dawe and Edna Longley (eds), *Across a Roaring Hill: The Protestant Imagination in Modern Ireland* (Belfast: Blackstaff, 1985), pp.99–123 (p.120).

56 Qtd in Norman Vance, *Irish Literature: A Social History* (Oxford: Oxford University Press, 1990), p.179.

57 St John Greer Ervine, *Sir Edward Carson and the Ulster Movement* (Dublin: Maunsel, 1915), p.122.

58 'St John Greer Ervine', CultureNorthernIreland, <http://www.culturenorthernireland. org/article/416/st-john-greer-ervine>, updated 15 April 2009, accessed 24 May 2014.

59 Auden and MacNeice, 'Last Will and Testament', p.252.

60 Geoffrey Grigson, 'Louis MacNeice', in *Recollection: Mainly of Writers and Artists* (London: Chatto and Windus, 1984), pp.72–6 (p.75). Letter of Louis MacNeice, *The Observer*, 2 February 1936, p.13, in response to a series of three articles by Ervine on the subject of 'Our Peevish Poets' beginning with the 29 December 1935 issue.

61 Louis MacNeice, 'Notes on the Way [2]', in *Time & Tide*, 33:28 (12 July 1952), pp.779–80; repr. in Alan Heuser (ed.), *Selected Prose of Louis MacNeice* (Oxford: Oxford University Press, 1990), p.181.

CHAPTER 3

The Apologies

W.H. Auden's Oxford tutor responded to the younger man's assertion he was going to be a poet with the observation that such a craft would improve Auden's prose. He was met by Auden's rebuke, 'You don't understand at all. I mean to be a great poet'.[1] Louis MacNeice was less certain about his calling when he arrived at Oxford a year later. He read Literae Humaniores – classics – and developed a comprehensive and highly skilled understanding of Greek and Roman literature and philosophy. At the same time, he published in the literary journal *The Cherwell*, edited the short-lived *Sir Galahad* (two issues 1928–29) and, with Stephen Spender, oversaw the 1929 edition of Blackwell's *Oxford Poetry*.

For a while, and encouraged by a close friendship with the young Anthony Blunt, MacNeice adopted the prevalent Oxbridge trope of Aestheticism and Pure Form, but he never quite pulled it off, and he found the classics a much more comfortable fit with their traditions of examining individual action in a world determined by fate, understandable in retrospect but seemingly capricious in the moment – Oedipus, for example, has no knowledge it is his father whom he slays and his mother whom he marries, yet he is punished for breaking those taboos. Additionally, his father's increasingly confident practice of witnessing the word of Christ regardless of societal expectations provided MacNeice a further template against which to test himself. Not surprisingly then, his three substantive studies of the role of art and artistry, *Modern Poetry* (1938), *The Poetry of W.B. Yeats* (1941) and the 1963 Clark Lectures published as *Varieties of*

Parable (1965) are all in some sense grounded in the venerable tradition of an 'apology' for one's life.

The apology genre began as a third-person justification with Plato's Απολογημα (apology) for Socrates's life and death and reached its apogee in the English tradition with the 1864 publication of John Henry Newman's *Apologia Pro Vita Sua*.[2] MacNeice's reviews and criticism show a man very much engaged with questions of personal integrity and communal responsibility. They offer, in effect, an extended apology for a life and the creative decisions that shaped it.

Surveying emerging trends in art in the second, and final, 1929 issue of *Sir Galahad*, MacNeice got to the heart of the paradox that 'the English have always liked "common sense" – facts which we can understand; but, as Hume showed, this leaves us paradoxically with nothing but feelings, which we can't'.[3] That definite article before 'English' suggests a degree of separation between MacNeice and those among whom he found himself – his father had entertained the notion that the University of Glasgow would have been a better fit for his son than Oxford – but the pronouns 'we' and 'us' re-connect him with the country where he was writing, while also universalising the human condition. MacNeice's life's work would be an extended discussion between 'an ideal[ism] working within an outlook (as distinct from a chaos) which is [an] outer convention' and an 'inner convention … usually called ⋯ "form"; the two should be concentric'.[4] Such concentric construction provided MacNeice the tools with which to address the ideal in the language of pragmatism. After all, 'a poet cannot live by style alone; nor even by intuition alone'.[5]

MacNeice asserted a claim to the importance of artistic integrity as a way of preserving individual identity in the midst of broader social concerns. It was an approach his father had espoused in specifically Christian terms: 'It is not the business of the Church to formulate schemes of reform … But it is the business of the Church to bear witness for the sacredness of human personality'.[6] Replace 'Church' with 'poetry' and you have a succinct summary of Louis's position. Like his father, Louis rejoiced that while 'people often speak as if the sole motive for all actions, whether of animals or human beings, were the wish to go on living, this is an inadequate explanation and not even a truly utilitarian one'.[7] Indeed,

One merely has to ask '*Why* should they wish to go on living?' and one introduces a question of value which has nothing to do with utility;

food may be useful because it keeps you alive but what is life useful for? The answer is that, if life is desirable, it is not desirable because it is useful but because it is good in itself … [it] is not something which you merely have or have not; it is something plastic; it *is* what you make it.[8]

How, then, to account for the creations of those living creatures? The obvious trap is Platonic, the idea that 'because a thing is in time its value can only be explained by an abstraction from the thing of some supposedly timeless quality … That a rose withers is no disproof of the rose',[9] but the idealist cannot explain the power of material things, how it is that

> The room was suddenly rich and the great bay-window was
> Spawning snow and pink roses against it
> Soundlessly collateral and incompatible:
> World is suddener than we fancy it.
>
> World is crazier and more of it than we think,
> Incorrigibly plural.[10]

Nonetheless, the answer cannot lie purely with the materialists, and 'human activity begins … with an urge which I can only describe as mystical'.[11]

Materialism and mysticism might appear to be an odd couple, but MacNeice's classics training and his understanding of his father's ability to balance faith in the immutable with the practical concerns of the mundane offered him the confidence to stake out this territory as his working area. Reviewing E.E. Sikes's *Lucretius, Poet and Philosopher*, MacNeice acknowledged that 'poetry and philosophy do not always work together in harmony, but they are not diametrically opposed'.[12] For the Epicurean Lucretius, philosophy was 'the mode which he deliberately employed in order to systematize his world (and his world involved his poetry)'.[13] That Lucretius's poetry was more than just philosophy put into stylised language is clear from the gap between Epicurus, in whose writing 'pity was left unexplained' and Lucretius's *De rerum natura* (on the nature of things), for there is 'plenty of pity in Lucretius'.[14]

Lucretius's poetry retained a compelling vitality centuries after it had been written, lost and rediscovered precisely because it had the sort of integrity MacNeice sought in rejecting 'the rarefying effects of good taste, and [I] have no sympathy with the idea that artists are people who should not soil their fingers with life. I don't agree that the style is the man'.[15] But as Lucretius showed, the man could be the making of the style.

In October 1940, resolved to return to Britain after a stay in the United States that had begun with him uncertain about the role he could or should play in the war, MacNeice acknowledged that

> The pity of it all
> Is all we compass if
> We watch disaster fall.

He could not ignore

> The watchers on the wall
> Awake all night who know
> The pity of it all.[16]

To a significant extent, it is 'pity' that separates the observant from the mere observer, and MacNeice's poetry, whatever formal devices he employed, was always an engagement with pity. The 'watchers on the wall' invoke the watchman who opens *The Agamemnon of Aeschylus*, a translation of which MacNeice had published in 1936: 'Fear stands by [the watchman] in the place of sleep', and he 'fall[s] to weeping for the fortunes of this house | Where not as before are things well ordered now'.[17] The reference also alludes to the third Isaiah and one of its post-exile oracular pronouncements: 'I have set watchmen upon thy walls, O Jerusalem, which shall never hold their peace day nor night.'[18] But if the poet were not to hold his peace, of what was he to speak?

Epicurus had started to question the underlying assumptions of his times at 'the age of twelve, when to his disgust his teachers could not explain to him the meaning of chaos'.[19] His solution had been to argue that although the 'natural order is unimaginably vast and complex it is nonetheless possible to understand something of its basic constitutive elements and its universal laws. Indeed, such understanding is one of human life's deepest pleasures'.[20] Although he would admit that 'the Epicurean ... [will not] burden his mind with facts *which cannot affect his own* life',[21] MacNeice always found meaning and often pleasure in the immediate that intimated the infinite, in the pity amid the chaos, precisely because the intimate and the infinite are connected in the immediate. Indeed, MacNeice saw the border between the theoretical and the practical as similar to the border between Northern Ireland and Éire, 'all very well for politicians ... but the ordinary Irishman on both sides, being a magnificent hypocrite and also basically practical, manages largely to ignore it'.[22] He was happy to adopt such a magnificent hypocrisy, not to mislead but to embrace the possibilities inherent in the incorrigibly plural.

MacNeice rejected relatively quickly the absolutist aesthetic attitude he had embraced on going up to Oxford. By the time he published *Modern Poetry*, sub-titled 'A Personal Essay', he was confident enough about the relationship between art and life to claim that 'the real escapist is the man who sits in his boat while keeping it moored to the bank'.[23] There is a 'distinction between the escape of a man who ... writes ... honest descriptions of anything he meets with in terms of his own experience, and the man who ... resorts to describing dreams which he has never met with'.[24]

Such a balance of 'art', 'escapism', and 'reality' meant that a 'poet is very intimately connected with his subject-matter' to such a degree that 'when the diction has out-lived the subject-matter it becomes a burden. New subject-matter therefore needs a new diction'.[25] MacNeice argued that while 'it is often brought against modern poets that their diction is not poetic enough' this was to miss the point.[26] As supporting evidence, he offered E.M. Forster on T.S. Eliot's 'Love Song of J. Alfred Prufrock' and 'Portrait of a Lady'. Forster had found them

> innocent of public-spiritedness: they sang of private disgust and diffidence, and of people who seemed genuine because they were unattractive or weak ... Here was a protest, and a feeble one, and the more congenial for being feeble. For what, in the world of gigantic horror, was tolerable except the slighter gestures of dissent? ... He who could turn aside to complain of ladies and drawing-rooms preserved a tiny drop of our self-respect, he carried on the human heritage.[27]

It is this sensibility that MacNeice argued informed the best of his contemporaries, who

> cannot be called optimists, for they see that there are always brute facts in opposition to their progress. But they should not be called

pessimists, for they see that, while on all sides there is a vast waste of
effort among human beings, to be able to waste effort like this implies
an astonishing fund of energy, and to be able to choose wrong so often
implies a capacity for choosing right. So when, as often, their poems
are gloomy, the gloom is tragic rather than defeatist.[28]

Such an attitude drove George Orwell to distraction:

What [MacNeice] wishes us to believe is that Eliot's 'successors'
(meaning Mr MacNeice and his friends) have in some way 'protested'
more effectively than Eliot did by publishing 'Prufrock' at the moment
when the Allied armies were assaulting the Hindenberg Line. Just
where those 'protests' are to be found I do not know.[29]

Orwell was not alone in finding MacNeice and his contemporaries
less engaged than they thought themselves to be. Julian Symons offered
the assessment in May 1940 that

belief in some external driving force outside himself and his own
feelings seems to be what is lacking to make Louis MacNeice a very
fine poet. He is wholly self-centered, stuck in a world in which the
virtues of the Ordinary Man are the cardinal virtues: generosity,
friendliness, physical love.[30]

That 'generosity, friendliness, physical love' are precisely why the 'Ordinary
Man' represented MacNeice's antidote to the 'pity' of grander schemes did
not stop Symons arguing that 'if MacNeice … is able to take the step of
adherence to some (not necessarily political) belief objective to himself,
that will probably be a good thing for him as a poet.'[31]

Perhaps part of the grounds for such a misreading was MacNeice's
distrust of rhetorical flourishes. MacNeice acknowledged that while Eliot's
'images are precise,'[32] the structural devices he employed often made his
poetry obscure or difficult, whatever its redeeming strengths in reclaiming
an interest in the individual experience. While MacNeice 'would not
dream of demanding that poets should not have tricks', and went so far
as to assert that 'any word is itself a trick', he advocated a poetry that used
'tricks … with discrimination and delicacy of touch. We should not "show
the works" and our tricks should be suited to our subject-matter.'[33] None

of which was to deny that either 'rhythm and rhyme' or 'diction', the topics of two of the chapters in *Modern Poetry*, should be different in poetry than in prose or drama, but those differences should have a purpose and be suited to the matter of the poem. Ultimately, MacNeice claimed that 'my own preference is for poetry which is musical but that the characteristics of this music are not superficial prettiness or smoothness, but (*a*) system and (*b*) significance'.[34]

This regard for 'system' and 'significance' contributed to what may be the most startling outburst in *Modern Poetry*, and perhaps in all of MacNeice's prose work:

> The poet needs to narrow his sphere. As everything may *in the long run* be relevant to everything else, there may always be a significance in the chance meeting of *x* and *y* on *z*. And, nearer home, there is always the possibility of comic relief in the juxtaposition of the unexpected. But the Unexpected does not wear well. We cannot make it the basis for poetry any more than we can make the practical joke a basis for conduct. F.H. Bradley in his 'Logic' states that every judgement is ultimately a judgement about the universe. But this does not mean that one judgement is not more important or more correct than another (in idealist philosophies, so often, we cannot see the trees for the wood). The poet, like the practical man, must presuppose a scale of values. Any odd set of words which any one uses may, on ultimate analysis, be significant, but the poet cannot wait for this ultimate. And, if he could, why should he bother to be a poet, seeing that the idiots in their institutions, the babies in their prams, can be just as significant without effort?[35]

The appropriate action of the poet is 'not merely to record a fact but to record a fact *plus*'.[36]

Poetry worth writing is 'true', but 'poetic truth is distinct from scientific truth. The poet ... gives [the reader] an amalgam which, if successful, represents truthfully his own relation to the world'.[37] Life has meaning but the problem of how to express that meaning was not so easily solved as to assert that it must be there, so the 'relationship between life and literature is almost impossible to analyse, but it should not be degraded into something like the translation of one language into another'.[38] The exceptions MacNeice offered were 'nonsense' poems such as those of

Edward Lear or Lewis Carroll, which had their own aesthetic and their own rationale. Nonetheless, MacNeice identified in Lear, who 'in spite of his loneliness … was always too frightened to ask anyone to marry him', a poet whose 'self-pity … is transmuted [in his poetry] – even in "The Yonghy-Bonghy-Bo" – and so ceases in fact to be self-pity'.[39] MacNeice had come a long way from admiration of Keats.

Just possibly, there was one other remarkable exception to this rule, and MacNeice addressed that when he turned his attention to William Butler Yeats, a poet who 'kept his questions comparatively simple and so was less likely to make hopelessly inadequate answers'.[40] This was not a statement of grudging respect, and throughout his work MacNeice stressed the difference between 'simple' questions, which can have rich and complex answers, and 'trivial' questions, which are hardly worth asking.[41] MacNeice might have underplayed the 'simplicity' of the questions both he and Yeats asked, but that didn't prevent him finding in Yeats's life an obvious corollary to his own: 'Ireland moulded Yeats's thoughts as a child', but it was London 'that influenced his earliest work'.[42] That tension helped create a foundation that enabled Yeats to be more than a poet of time and place. Looking back on his career, Yeats acknowledged the influence the Young Ireland movement had had on him. 'This is a startling admission', MacNeice wrote. 'There can be few great poets who in their adult years were inspired by such bad poetry.'[43] But Yeats himself had noted that if the Young Ireland poets 'had something else to write about besides political opinions, if more of them would write about the beliefs of the people … or about old legends … they would find it easier *to get a style*'.[44] The italics are MacNeice's.

Yeats reached this attitude after participating in an extensive print debate about the nature of poetry done well. MacNeice had objections to both sides of the debate, instinctively distrusting anything with an either / or option, but his objection to Yeats's stance at this point of his own development is revealing. Yeats, MacNeice noted, 'at this period habitually assumed a false separation between spiritual and physical; he did not see that in that in-between world, which is the world of both poetry and normal life, they are as closely related as convex to concave'.[45] He welcomed the older poet's eventual dual rejection of an aestheticism inspired by Walter Pater and of poetry 'in which there is not an athletic joy',[46] but the younger man thought this did not go far enough. Yeats had found this sensibility exemplified in Lady Gregory and the 'Big House', but it was a 'snob idyllicism'[47] that 'ignored the fact that in most cases these houses maintained no culture worth speaking of – nothing but an obsolete bravado, an insidious bonhomie and a way with horses'.[48] No wonder Yeats described MacNeice as 'an extreme radical' in a 1935 letter to Dorothy Wellesley.[49]

Nonetheless, 'athletic joy' – whatever its associated problems – was a mind-set whose importance MacNeice underscored when welcoming the birth of his son, Dan, in 1934. He wished him to

> accumulate, corroborate while he may
> The blessedness of fact
> Which lives in the dancing atom and the breathing trees
> And everywhere except in the fancy of man
> Who daubs his slush on the hawthorn and the may.[50]

Wondering how to play the role of parent, MacNeice recapitulated what he saw as the poet's obligation, which was the obligation of all those who would embrace life, vowing to remain 'mystic and maudlin', to 'dream of both real and ideal'.[51]

Yeats began in his later poetry, said MacNeice, to model those syntheses the new father espoused, embracing the 'world as a whole of parts in which the parts must neither usurp the whole nor be merely merged in it'.[52] Whatever is undertaken in this spirit 'absolves the man of action from the vulgar motivation of mere animal spirits or merely mechanical necessity',[53] offering recognition of MacNeice's insistence that life must have a purpose. Lurking behind that analysis is the spectre that would always haunt MacNeice: Action without pity is reckless in its disregard of its consequences, and the danger is that we come to

> envy men of action
> Who sleep and wake, murder and intrigue
> Without being doubtful, without being haunted.[54]

Yeats's 'philosophy of antinomies' meant that as his poetry became more energetic, more aware of its devices and its impulses, it became 'a dialogue where [Yeats] himself does all the talking'.[55]

Yeats's poetry improved over time, MacNeice suggested, in part because practice tends to improve any craft and in part because Yeats's understanding of his self-identity deepened. Such improvement, however, did not necessarily make Yeats a better person, even if it made his poetry more honest. By the time he wrote 'Sailing to Byzantium', in which MacNeice found much to admire, Yeats had developed 'an inhuman Greek admiration for humanity and even enjoyed seeing human beings *hamper* each other … apparent frustration and failure [being] part of the eternal process'.[56] MacNeice called out 'the pity of it, [which] is that the frustrated and the men who fail cannot themselves see the logic – or the harmony – of their own misfortunes'.[57] But then, as MacNeice admitted, ending the chapter with the assertion and leaving the reader to absorb the implications of the observation, Yeats 'was [not] much worried by pity'.[58]

In recognising the central role of pity, MacNeice had already established his 'adherence to some belief objective to himself', whatever Symons had thought, and ultimately this gave him something close to a faith to draw upon throughout his writing. 'I'm afraid I can't take philosophy seriously yet, being obsessed by my own little games of stitching words together', he had written to Blunt during the summer of 1928.[59] 'To be a philosopher you have to really doubt everything and I only pretend to doubt.'[60] Yet not doubting certain foundational axioms did not mean one had all the answers, and part of the joy of life was that

> All we know is the splash of words in passing
> > And falling twigs of song,
> And when we try to eavesdrop on the great
> > Presences it is rarely
> That by a stroke of luck we can appropriate
> > Even a phrase entirely.[61]

Which is a cause of joy because 'if the world were black or white entirely …'

> We might be surer where we wished to go
> > Or again we might be merely
> Bored but in brute reality there is no
> > Road that is right entirely.[62]

MacNeice would continue to publish observations and thoughts on poetry, and would provide some occasional commentary on his own volumes, but his only other sustained work of criticism was his 1963 Clark Lectures. The twenty-two years between publication of the Yeats book and the lectures meant MacNeice had accumulated experiences, personal and professional, that changed the tools and perspective he brought to mediating truth through experience, but his underlying principles had remained intact, reinforced by a depth of practice and of reading:

> Desmond Pacey, who dined with MacNeice at the Trinity high table after each lecture, records his own surprise at MacNeice's serious interest in allegory: 'His lectures dealing with the element of parable in English literature were thoroughly prepared and revealed that MacNeice had read and pondered all the major works of modern criticism … I made some reference to the amount of reading he must have had to do in preparing the lectures, and he informed me a little testily that he would have read all the books anyway'.[63]

In his introductory remarks to the book of the lectures, MacNeice once again asserted that while they are connected, 'as every poet knows, one cannot draw any clear line between form and content'.[64] In thinking about how English audiences responded to Dante and to John Bunyan he underscored his argument that

> in poetry the formal elements are part of the meaning or the content, [and] I would add at this point that the content, which includes of course any beliefs expressed in a poem, must *ipso facto* – at least if the poem is to be valid – have a part in the shaping of that poem. Which means that in this respect the beliefs are formalizing elements.[65]

Reading the poems from MacNeice's middle years, which so many readers and critics have largely dismissed, we should consider that the 'formal elements' are not mere experiments in style; rather, they reflect his understanding that

> In the 1930's we used to say that the poet should contain the journalist; now I would tend more often to use 'contain' in the sense of control or limit. I still hold that a poet should look at, feel about and think about

the world around him, but he should not suppose his job consists merely in reporting on it. What the poet is far more concerned with is that 'inner conflict' mentioned by [C.S.] Lewis [in *The Allegory of Love*] which he said requires metaphorical writing.[66]

In offering these remarks, MacNeice was specifically contrasting his claims to those of the 'Movement' poets, of whom Philip Larkin was the most prominent. 'One often hears people nowadays – and I agree with them', MacNeice wrote, 'regretting the deficiency of myth in modern poetry'.[67] The exact definition of 'myth' is problematic and 'if the word is used strictly … [it] is something that the will cannot supply, for it has to be given or rather inherited'.[68] In the end, MacNeice offered 'parable' as the most functional word to describe his interests, but the idea that there should be a component of poetry that is 'mystical', the word he had favoured in his study of Yeats, had not changed.

If never a poet of unadulterated realism, MacNeice argued that with the century now past its midpoint 'realism in the photographic sense is almost played out and no longer satisfies our needs'.[69] The crucial word here is 'needs', with its bundled complexity of meanings, both social and individual, and its invocation both of desire and of a more profound necessity. The medieval Everyman plays and their portrait of the archetypal human 'searching for truth and finding it or losing it' offered MacNeice a touchstone.[70] He found strength in the validating nature of that search, with its recognition of the inherent pity of an unfulfillable quest justified by intention rather than by experience. It was a trope that allowed for the 'athletic' writing Yeats had urged and for a poem's demonstration of 'the virtues of good prose',[71] for which Eliot had called. It was why MacNeice could find perhaps surprising connections between Edmund Spenser's *The Faerie Queene* and William Wordsworth's 'Resolution and Independence', which 'although approached from a quite new direction … is very like Spenser country – which means an internal country', and, as with Spenser, 'if you use the versification touchstone, you will find that the form is properly matched to the content, that the two are so wedded that they are one body – and one soul'.[72]

In concluding his lectures, MacNeice considered William Golding's novel *Pincher Martin*. Martin, 'like many of the heroes in modern parable writing, is much concerned with his own identity'.[73] Pincher's story is an unpeeling of an onion, and while 'if you strip the onion to pieces you will probably not find a heart … if you know all those layers upon layers, you may with luck put the onion together again; this is not possible in horticulture but it is, I suggest, both in art and in human life'.[74]

MacNeice might as well have been talking about his own body of work.

NOTES

References to the poems of Louis MacNeice are as they appear in Peter McDonald (ed.), *Collected Poems* (London: Faber, 2007), except as noted.

1   Humphrey Carpenter, *W.H. Auden: A Biography* (Boston, MA: Houghton Mifflin, 1981), p.54.
2   John Henry Newman, *Apologia Pro Vita Sua: Being a Reply to a Pamphlet Entitled 'What Then Does Dr Newman Mean?'* (London, 1864).
3   Louis MacNeice, 'Our God Bogus', *Sir Galahad*, 2 (14 May 1929); repr. in Alan Heuser (ed.), *Selected Prose of Louis MacNeice* (Oxford: Oxford University Press, 1990), pp.1–7 (p.6).
4   Ibid.
5   Louis MacNeice, *The Poetry of W.B. Yeats* (Oxford: Oxford University Press, 1941; repr. London: Faber, 1967), p.31.
6   John Frederick MacNeice, 'Peace through Goodwill: Bishop's Christmas Message, 1936', in John Frederick MacNeice, *Our First Loyalty* (Belfast: Erskine Mayne, 1937), pp.104–7 (pp.104–5).
7   MacNeice, *Yeats*, p.23.
8   Ibid., pp.23–4.
9   Ibid., p.15.
10 Louis MacNeice, 'Snow', p.24.
11 MacNeice, *Yeats*, p.24.
12 Louis MacNeice, 'The Passionate Unbeliever', rev. of *Lucretius, Poet and Philosopher* by E.E. Sikes (Cambridge: Cambridge University Press, 1936), *The Spectator*, 5628 (8 May 1936), p.846; repr. in *Selected Prose*, pp.20–22 (p.20).
13 Ibid., pp.20–1.
14 Ibid., p.21.
15 Louis MacNeice, 'In Defence of Vulgarity', BBC National Programme, 20 December 1937; repr. in *The Listener*, 18:468 (29 December 1937), pp.1407–8; repr. in *Selected Prose*, pp.43–8 (pp.46–7).
16 Louis MacNeice, 'Cradle Song for Eleanor', p.209.
17 Louis MacNeice, *The Agamemnon of Aeschylus* (London: Faber, 1936), pp.13–14.
18 Isaiah 62:6.
19 Stephen Greenblatt, *The Swerve: How the World became Modern* (New York, NY: Norton, 2011), p.74.
20 Ibid.

21 Louis MacNeice, *Modern Poetry: A Personal Essay* (London: Oxford University Press, 1938), p.88. [Italics in the original.]

22 Louis MacNeice, 'Talking about Rugby', *New Statesman*, 57:149 (28 February 1959), pp.286–8; repr. in *Selected Prose*, pp.214–16 (p.214).

23 MacNeice, *Modern Poetry*, p.7.

24 Ibid.

25 Ibid., p.139.

26 Ibid.

27 E.M. Forster, *Abinger Harvest* (London: Edward Arnold, 1936), p.88; qtd in MacNeice, *Modern Poetry*, p.12. [The ellipses are MacNeice's.]

28 MacNeice, *Modern Poetry*, p.16.

29 George Orwell, 'Inside the Whale', in *The Collected Essays, Journalism and Letters of George Orwell* Vol. 1, *An Age Like This: 1920–1940*, ed. Sonia Orwell and Ian Angus (London: Secker and Warburg, 1968), pp.493–526 (p.524).

30 Julian Symons, 'Louis MacNeice: The Artist as Everyman', *Poetry*, 56:11 (May 1940), pp.86–94 (p.92).

31 Ibid., p.94.

32 MacNeice, *Modern Poetry*, p.103.

33 Ibid., pp.149–50.

34 Ibid., p.134.

35 Ibid., p.159. MacNeice is referring to *The Principles of Logic* by F. H. Bradley (New York: Stechert, 1912). For more on Bradley, see, Stewart Candlish and Pierfrancesco Basile, 'Francis Herbert Bradley', *The Stanford Encyclopedia of Philosophy* (spring 2013 Edition), ed. Edward N. Zalta, <http://plato.stanford.edu/archives/spr2013/entries/bradley/>, updated spring 2013, accessed 30 June 2014.

36 MacNeice, *Modern Poetry*, p.197. [Italics in the original.]

37 Ibid.

38 Ibid., p.198.

39 Edward Lear, 'The Courtship of The Yonghy-Bonghy-Bo', in *Laughable Lyrics. A Fourth Book of Nonsense Poems, Songs, Botany, Music, &c.* (London: 1877), pp.21–6; Louis MacNeice,*Varieties of Parable* (Cambridge: Cambridge University Press, 1965), p.19.

40 MacNeice, *Yeats*, p.30.

41 Ibid.

42 Ibid., p.32.

43 Ibid., p.55.

44 Ibid., p.75. [The italics are MacNeice's.]

45 Ibid., p.87.

46 William Butler Yeats to AE [George Russell], ? April 1904, in *The Collected Letters of W.B. Yeats* Volume 3, *1901 to 1904*, gen. ed., John Kelly, eds, John Kelly and Ronald Schuchard (Oxford: Oxford University Press, 1994), p.578, cited in MacNeice, *Yeats*, p.82.

47 MacNeice, *Yeats*, p.82.

48 Ibid., p.97.

49 William Butler Yeats to Dorothy Violet Wellesley (Lady Gerald Wellesley), 20 October 1935, in Dorothy Wellesley (ed.), *Letters on Poetry from W.B. Yeats to Dorothy Wellesley* (London: Oxford University Press, 1940), p.39.

50   Louis MacNeice, 'Ode', pp.32–7 (p.33).

51   Ibid., p.37.

52   MacNeice, *Yeats*, p.99.

53   Ibid.

54   Louis MacNeice, *Autumn Journal*, XVI, p.137.

55   MacNeice, *Yeats*, p.126.

56   Ibid., p.139. [Italics in the original.]

57   Ibid.

58   Ibid.

59   Louis MacNeice to Anthony Blunt, [22 August 1928], p.194.

60   Ibid.

61   Louis MacNeice, 'Entirely', p.171.

62   Ibid.

63   Terence Brown, 'Louis MacNeice and the "Dark Conceit"', *Ariel,* 3:4 (October 1972), pp.16–24 (p.16), quoting Desmond Pacey, 'The Dance Above the Dazzling Wave', *Transactions of the Royal Society of Canada*, vol. iii, ser. iv (June 1965), pp.147–63 (pp.152–3).

64   MacNeice, *Varieties*, p.5.

65   Ibid., p.19.

66   Ibid., p.8.

67   MacNeice, *Varieties*, p.3.

68   Ibid.

69   Ibid., p.26.

70   Ibid., p.29.

71   T.S. Eliot, 'Introduction', in *Johnson's 'London' and 'The Vanity of Human Wishes'* (London: Haslewood, 1930), pp.9–17; repr. in Phylis M. Jones (ed.), *English Critical Essays: Twentieth Century* (London: Oxford University Press, 1947), pp.301–10.

72   MacNeice, *Varieties*, p.71.

73   Ibid., p.151.

74   Ibid.

CHAPTER 4

The Ladies of His Life Lingered

In December 1962, Louis MacNeice told his sister that 'you and I, Elizabeth, remember so much about our childhoods, yet we seem to remember such different things'.[1] It is perhaps a little glib to suggest those differences offer a key to understanding his life and writing, but the significantly different ways the siblings recalled their mother provide some inkling into the source of one consistent trope in his writing: the importance of instinct and generosity.

The differences in memory between Louis and Elizabeth were deep-rooted and are hinted at in her choice of a title for her discussion of their childhoods. She turned to the opening line of his poem 'Autobiography', that had by then become the seminal poem critics used to approach her brother's relationship with memory, loss and rejection, with its refrain after every couplet calling on his mother to *'Come back early or never come'*.[2] The poem is built around the removal of his mother, Lily, to a nursing home in Dublin shortly before his sixth birthday. She would die there of tuberculosis in December 1914, her children not having seen her after she left the rectory in Carrickfergus. For the title of her piece reflecting on this period, Elizabeth selected her brother's opening observation that 'In my childhood trees were green | And there was plenty to be seen.'[3] This was a memory of the rectory at Carrickfergus, whence the family moved when he was three. 'I have never forgotten the thrill of surprise on the first morning when I woke up to the dawn chorus', Elizabeth recalled. The family was 'suddenly … in another world with a lawn to play on, trees to climb, and a garden which seemed to be full of apple-blossom'.[4]

Importantly, their mother was 'very pleased by this move. All her instincts were of the country and she began at once enlarging the henyard, planting trees, acquiring cats and dogs and hens ... The house ticked with the seasons.'[5]

Lily MacNeice was the daughter of Church of Ireland mission school parents. Her husband found in the Bible very specific guidance to approaching matters of morality and, increasingly, a guide to separating the spiritual from the secular so that he would, incrementally, come to advocate a position bordering on quietism while managing to make that stance hold up a mirror to the inequities and corruptions of society, a shining example of the virtues that should have found more frequent expression in a church that had been disestablished and needed no longer to be beholden to political currents. He was, his son would say, a 'generous puritan,'[6] but much of that generosity found expression through his wife, who retained an affection for 'the traditional ceremonies. We picked mayflowers on May eve, we rolled eggs in the field on Easter Monday, my mother taught us all the Hallowe'en games and provided the right foods.'[7] It was a household where faith was not separated from the sensual but informed it. Their mother 'was always thinking of enchanting things to do with us ... I remember, too, how her feet never failed to tap to a dance tune.'[8] Those were the days, said his sister, when 'if I had to find an epigram to sum it up ... I think it would be "Hadn't we the gaiety"'.[9]

But 'hadn't we the gaiety' is a statement inevitably imbued with a sense of loss and of yearning, and for Louis it would be a yearning and a sense of loneliness bordering on fear that shaped his dominant memories of childhood: 'When I woke they did not care; | Nobody, nobody was there.'[10] Whatever the retrospective dramatisation, the fact remains that for the youngest child in the rectory the departure and then death of his mother represented a rift between promise and reality he could never reconcile. The gaiety Louis had known as a young child was channelled through his mother. The changes that came to the rectory with her illness and departure underscored the power of women to tame and nurture the otherwise frightening.

One constant throughout Louis's life was his sister, although once they started their education in England they were apart more often than not. Elizabeth left for school some months before him and her absence added to his sense of loneliness and separation, but she also provided reassurance that departure from Carrickfergus would open horizons. She

preceded her brother to Dorset and then to Oxford, where she attended
St Hugh's College, graduating with a degree in physiology in 1925 before
completing her medical studies in 1932. Her choice of career was not
merely intellectual curiosity. She and Louis had a brother, Willie, who
had Down's syndrome and Elizabeth's first position after completing her
training demonstrated her deep personal motivation for pursuing her
degree: she started work at the Tavistock Institute of Medical Psychology.
Now part of the Tavistock and Portman NHS Foundation Trust, the 'Tavi',
as it was known, was founded in the aftermath of the First World War
by Hugh Crichton-Miller to treat patients in a manner based at least in
part on his experience working with shell-shock sufferers. The 'Tavi' was
committed to 'de-medicalis[ing] a patient's experience, so there were no
beds, no medical equipment and no white coats. This was highly unusual
at the time, and it remains a feature of the trust today that it does not feel
like a medical institution, and one cannot easily tell staff from patients'.[11]
Louis would spend much of life looking forward to a world changed for
the better; his sister engaged in trying to bring about such changes.

While studying at Oxford, Elizabeth started a relationship with a
medical student that would last a lifetime. John Nicholson was the son of
Sir Charles Archibald Nicholson, who was appointed church architect of
St Anne's Cathedral, Belfast, in 1924 – he designed the west front of the
cathedral. Elizabeth's marriage brought her connections that helped foster
the patience her younger brother required of her as, later in life, he took
to leaving his son, Dan, in her care, often with an accompanying nanny,
or otherwise embarking on adventures she considered at least partially
ill-conceived. Her mother-in-law was Evelyn Olivier, aunt of Laurence
Olivier, and her father-in-law's brothers were Archibald Nicholson, the
stained-glass artist, and Sir Sydney Nicholson, organist and master of
the choristers of Westminster Abbey and founder of the Royal School of
Church Music.

Nicholson was a standout medical student, winning the 1929 Willett
Medal for the highest marks in operative surgery at the Brackenbury
Surgical Examination at St Bartholomew's Hospital, whence he earned
his degree the same year. Among the London hospitals where he served
as a consultant was the National Temperance Hospital, which provided
another connection between the two families, Elizabeth and Louis's father
had once undertaken the formidable task of creating a teetotal Orange
lodge in the heart of East Belfast. In 1934 Nicholson became a fellow of

the Royal College of Surgeons and during the war served in the Royal Army Medical Corps as a surgical specialist. Elizabeth also served during the war as a doctor in the Emergency Medical Services. She would spend some period of time in Plymouth working with those injured, physically and mentally, by bombing raids on the docks and docklands area, and while there she also worked at Plymouth Mental Hospital, the psychiatric hospital known as Moorhaven Psychiatric Hospital from 1947 until its closure. On his father's death, Nicholson inherited the baronetcy of Luddenham, a title bestowed on his grandfather, a surgeon and first chancellor of the University of Sydney in Australia who had also been the first president of the Queensland Legislative Council. But for all the trappings and access to influence, Sir John, like his wife and his father-in-law, was perhaps happiest where he could do most good. Returning from Harvard University, where he had gone soon after the war as a fellow in surgery, he chose to practice in the first years of the National Health Service in the East London Group of hospitals.

Both his brother-in-law and sister shared with Louis a reserve behind which lay great warmth and a keen understanding of the human condition:

> John Nicholson was a character and at first sight a formidable one. He was in reality a sensitive man with a warm and generous heart whose integrity was absolute. Those who knew him well appreciated these qualities, as did many of his patients in the East End: They realised that he felt as warmly to them as they did to him ... He was essentially a practical man who had an educated and well furnished mind, a combination that made him a good companion.[12]

Shortly before Elizabeth's death, Ian and Carole Dow moved into the house opposite Thames Cottage in Sunbury-on-Thames, where the Nicholsons had made their home after retirement. They remembered her as 'elegant, very formal, polite and distant, but at a party she gave where she stood apart for much of the time she also had a wonderful smile that we noticed more than once'.[13] Geoffrey Grigson found her as 'pale as [Louis] was dark, and even more remote'.[14]

At the end of her brother's life, too late to help him because of his stubbornness, Elizabeth took charge of Louis's medical care and moved him to St Leonard's Hospital, Shoreditch, where her husband was still practicing. Fittingly, then, although he died in hospital, Louis MacNeice essentially died cared for and looked after by the sister who had always offered him love and understanding and who saved her rebukes of him for private moments and private letters.

Elizabeth spent much time in her final years gathering together MacNeice family material, but when she died in a car crash returning home one night in 1981 the papers were still uncatalogued and their future undetermined. Her husband's health declined after her death and he died five years later, leaving his property to the couple who had taken care of the house and garden after Elizabeth's death. They sold the house and burnt material they conceived as having no value, including the papers Elizabeth had so carefully gathered. Elizabeth barely appears in her brother's poetry, yet much of it would not have been written had she not unfailingly been there to reassure him that the 'gaiety' had been real and to offer a refuge when he needed.

While an undergraduate at Oxford, MacNeice never quite fit in with those entirely focused on the aesthetic life so successfully satirised in *Brideshead Revisited*,[15] but he sympathised with the main principle of Walter Pater's argument that 'it is great passion … and especially the "poetic passion" that give us a quickened sense of life.'[16] And so, when he met Giovanna Marie Thérèse Babette Ezra, known as Mary, the stepdaughter of the great classicist John Davidson Beazley, he was immediately stricken. She

> looked as fragile as porcelain and measured her life by dance-cards kept in a lavendered box tied with a ribbon. Said to be the best dancer in Oxford, she was in great demand … When not dancing with one of her beaux, she was usually to be found 'lying on a sofa covered with Moorish embroideries as if she would never sit upright, much less stand, again. She said standing made her feel faint.'[17]

MacNeice 'did not dance',[18] but he successfully wooed Ezra and they married despite the opposition of both sets of parents.

After graduating, he moved to Birmingham University and a position as an assistant lecturer in classics. It was a move 'that humanised his aestheticism',[19] albeit gradually. In Birmingham, all seemed to start well: Louis and Mary lived in a converted stable 'where they played an endless game of "keeping house" … an Enchanted Island where the two of them would live happy ever after'.[20] This was the grown-up version of the great game of make-believe he and Elizabeth had created after the departure of their mother, when they had claimed descent from the Great Queen Mac Niss and had established in their rectory garden a court for her and her fantastical companions. In the midst of that second great period of game playing, Charles Katzman, an American graduate student who had been befriended by Ezra's mother, entered the enchanted island. He had 'the charm of a shaggy sheepdog who expects to be laughed at. Although his voice too was shaggy and he spoke very slowly he and [Mary] understood each other at once'.[21]

MacNeice and Katzman shared adventures appropriate in retrospect to the decay of the island's charm. He crashed his car on a drive with Katzman, walking home after coming-to, only to discover that Katzman had been taken to hospital from the scene of the accident – an account which raises all sorts of questions either about MacNeice's telling or about the quality of England's roadside emergency services in 1935. Soon after, MacNeice sprained an ankle and had to walk for a while with two canes. Katzman left Birmingham for London and the real world in early November, and, as if to underscore the changes required after one grows up and has a child, on 18 November 1935 the converted stable rooms caught fire. MacNeice 'carefully changed my trousers [before I] got our landlady's long-handled axe and smashed the cement base of the hearth' to gain access to the beams underneath that were burning.[22] He was, he said, 'in the height of never-again don't care-spirits'.[23] The next morning, Ezra left for London, 'there to join [Katzman] and not to come back again. She told me later it was because she was "lonely in her mind."'[24]

Following Ezra's departure, MacNeice had a highly productive period – much of it the culmination of work he had started earlier – for, whatever his distractions or professional obligations, writing remained always something he did and, more importantly, worked at. But he grew tired of Birmingham and headed for London, taking a position at Bedford College, one of the women's colleges of the University of London. By then, he had a reputation as a rising star of the new literary order and friendships he had developed throughout his public school and university education offered him introductions to the sprawling arts culture of London. His long-standing friendship with W.H. Auden also resulted in MacNeice meeting Nancy Coldstream, née Sharp. She was married to William Coldstream, who had temporarily given up painting to work, like Auden, in the GPO Film Unit.[25] Sharp, too, was painting very little as she was raising their two daughters, Juliet and Miranda. Auden lodged with the Coldstreams and a friendship developed between the three of them, with Auden often bringing his own friends back to the London flat. By the time MacNeice moved to London he knew the Coldstreams well enough that they travelled north to his farewell-to-Birmingham party on 26 September 1936.

Sharp was the daughter of a Cornish surgeon who shared with Elizabeth's husband 'a particular sweet nature … As a doctor he was superb – he had a natural warmth although somewhat severe'.[26] Sharp's own childhood memories shared something with MacNeice, too. She was part of 'a very happy family … although I was v[ery] miserable a lot of the time for being left out'. Her older brother and sister were close and had many friends in the area, but Nancy 'had almost no one my age and this my mother found very tiresome … I was always late for everything and I can still hear my mother's sharp voice saying "we shall leave you behind if you are not ready Nancy". Luck was seldom with me'.[27]

MacNeice had first been introduced to Sharp in early 1936 at the Café Royal, a favourite spot of many contemporary artists, regardless of specific allegiance, as Anthony Powell intimated when sketching the relationship between the two fictional writers Mark Members and J.G. Quiggin:

> Members … had been heard complaining that he himself was in sympathy with 'with all liberal and progressive movements', but 'J.G. had advanced into a state of mind too political to be understood by civilised people'. In spite of such differences, and reported statements of both of them that they 'rarely saw each other now', they were not uncommonly to be found together, arguing or sulking on the banquettes of the Café Royal.[28]

'Louis came to dinner on many occasions,' Sharp recalled later. 'On one of these Louis, Bill [Coldstream] and Wystan [Auden] began an argument as to who had the finest hair. Both Louis and Wystan were sure their hair was the finest so eventually the hair of each was examined and Bill [was] pronounced the winner – an outcome which annoyed everyone.'[29] Sharp had been 'fascinated by the length and lustre of the black locks that Louis unwound like a Sikh's turban'.[30]

MacNeice's marriage had ended and Sharp's relationship with Coldstream was ragged, and the two of them started to see more of each other. Sometime in the autumn of 1936, 'MacNeice came across [Nancy] pushing her pram back from Hampstead Heath and they stopped and talked. His "black velvet voice" brought to her mind a sentence from Isaiah, "Aha, I am warm, I have seen the fire".[31] By the next year they were having an affair, enabled, at least in part, by her husband's apparent agreement with Auden's observation that MacNeice 'could be very convenient', entertaining Sharp while her husband painted.[32] MacNeice was also a source of encouragement for her:

> I remember some time later having coffee with him in the Café Royal. I was gloomy because I wanted to get on with my painting and drawing and was bogged down in domestic chores. Louis got v enthusiastic and told me to go somewhere like Iceland or Greenland for 3 weeks and write a book and illustrate it ... By the end of the evening I was convinced that I could do anything.[33]

Together, they went to the Hebrides and collaborated on *I Crossed the Minch*, a trip she recalled many years later for the BBC programme 'A Gift of Autumn'.[34] Later, in London, they collaborated on *Zoo*, a book they had intended to be 'a few words and a drawing on each page', but this was 'too expensive'. Nonetheless, they had 'great fun ... looking at the animals and having picnics in the zoo'.[35] His encouragement of her work also convinced Sharp to try painting his portrait, although she

> had never painted a portrait before and was full of misgivings. But I did it. I painted Louis looking broody, with his black hair and his shiny fisherman's black mac with the velvet collar. He sat in the attic afternoon after afternoon until it was finished – and afterwards he was pleased with the result ... It was hung next to [a portrait of King] George VI in the Royal Academy – to our mutual amusement; and later on shown in Dublin – where it was well received – and in the Ulster Museum.[36]

At some stage, Sharp realised that, whatever the state of her marriage, a long-term relationship with Louis was likely to be a mistake: 'His lack of interest in children – hers included – she found troubling'.[37] Her relationship with MacNeice fizzled as the war loomed but remained such that at the party to celebrate the April 1941 marriage of Stephen Spender and Natasha Litvin, Spender noted that 'among the guests were ... Louis

MacNeice and Nancy Coldstream.'³⁸ Connected by the conjunction and separated from other attendees by commas, they seem to have come to the wedding as a couple, and, indeed, while the Spenders 'spent the first night of their honeymoon at the Savoy Hotel they were telephoned a number of times during the night by an intoxicated Louis MacNeice and Nancy Coldstream, engaged in less legitimate lovemaking'.³⁹

Sharp's relationship with her husband steadily disintegrated. They tried to make a fresh start in 1939 but that attempt failed sometime in autumn that year, unrelated to the outbreak of hostilities. 'They tried again later, maybe more than once', but to no avail.⁴⁰ Soon after apparently ending things with MacNeice, Sharp had a brief affair with Michael Spender, brother of Stephen. This relationship resumed and faltered again in 1939, but in 1940 their relationship became more stable. Although their respective divorces would not come through until 1942 (Sharp) and early 1943 (Spender), Sharp's marriage with Coldstream had essentially ended by the end of 1940 or January 1941 when she and Spender moved into 30 Upper Park Road, near Belsize Park. They married in March 1943. Their son was born the same year.

A squadron leader in the Royal Air Force and an expert on aerial photography, Spender was injured in a crash over Germany on 3 May 1945 and died two days later. He was on 'a flight ... which wasn't officially sanctioned, and it was the day more or less that the Armistice was declared, and the Army then refused to accept responsibility ... And so [Nancy] was left as a widow and pretty well impoverished'.⁴¹ Spender could be 'often arrogant and tactless',⁴² but Sharp 'took years to recover from the blow'⁴³ of his death as the two had natures seemingly well suited to each other. She was 'pugnacious, mischievous, and occasionally snobbish. She didn't suffer fools gladly and enjoyed the occasional scrap'.⁴⁴ There was something similar between the way she was regarded later in life and descriptions of MacNeice at the BBC: 'She was treated with respect by most, with circumspection by all, and held in awe by the occasional newcomer'.⁴⁵ Sharp also had a sense of humour that leavened her sometimes disarmingly frank comments, as when she concluded a long letter written in the first two weeks of the war to John Auden, Wystan's older brother who was a geologist with the Geological Survey of India, with the scribbled post script: 'Do you like this letter or is it too long? Anyway, read it because it is kinder and more polite, yes? Airmail is now 1/3d instead [of] 1½ᵈ per ½oz! So see how I love you.'⁴⁶

Sharp responded to her husband's death with 'characteristic determination ... teaching art [and] taking no nonsense from her pupils during 10 years at [the Archbishop Temple School in Lambeth] a tough south London school'.[47] It was only in the late 1970s that she started exhibiting her work again, leading one gallery owner to suggest she may well have been 'the most underrated artist of her generation'.[48]

When MacNeice's relationship with Sharp began to shift to one that was both calmer and imbued in part with nostalgia for the last summer of peace, he headed to the United States and was introduced to the group of writers around the *Partisan Review*. Once again, he threw himself into a relationship. This one, with Eleanor Clark, was perhaps both the least practical and the least likely of his long-term partnerships. Clark's family had a rich cultural heritage and she once observed that 'We have [Henry Wadsworth] Longfellow's quill pen from my grandfather. I was very irked because my mother gave that pen to my husband instead of me – she didn't really take women writers seriously'.[49] During her junior year at Vassar College she had established *The Housatonic* with three other students. Named after the town in Connecticut where her parents then lived, the idea was 'to work, through a critical survey of New England economics, politics, social conditions, and culture, past and present, to a positive view for the future'.[50] This was a manifesto not dissimilar to those in Britain which MacNeice had distrusted for putting art at the service of politics. Also at Vassar, Clark might have teamed up with Elizabeth Bishop, among others, on the journal *Con Spirito*, a name picked by Bishop for 'its pun joining the musical notation meaning "with zest" to the announcement of a conspiracy'.[51] Publishing anonymously, the journal's staff reputedly met in a speakeasy, offering another pun on the word 'spirito'.[52] This would have been an activity more in line with MacNeice's temperament.

Clark was outspoken in support of the League of Nations and disarmament, and before MacNeice met her she had married and divorced Jan Frankel, a former private secretary of Leon Trotsky. Most accounts reckon the marriage was one of convenience to allow Frankel, born of Jewish parents in what was then the Austro-Hungarian Empire, to acquire a US passport. It was a gesture MacNeice would have understood and sympathised with; he was well aware of Auden's 1935 marriage to Erika Mann, Thomas Mann's daughter, in order to secure her a British passport. In 1936, he had participated in a similar wedding of the novelist John Simpson, who wrote under the pseudonym John Hampson, and Therese

Giehse, a friend of Erika Mann. 'What are buggers for?' Auden reputedly asked Simpson when selling his friend on the scheme.[53] When she met MacNeice in New York in 1939, Clark was once again single, loudly vivacious and deeply engaged in intellectual left-wing circles. MacNeice returned to London, sent letter after letter to Clark expressing his sincere and passionate love for her – reading the letters one can see why Sharp had come to find him overwhelming – apparently oblivious to her reticence about a physical relationship and ignoring his own continuing meetings with Sharp. He would return to the States in January 1940 motivated by an intense ambivalence about the war, an inability to find permanent refuge in Éire and a desire to see and seduce Clark.

Their reunion was fraught from the start. Clark challenged the reticence she found in *Autumn Journal*, appreciating both the structural skill and the overall sense of concern for humanity, but cavilling at the lack of a call for political action. The pre-war period she would recall as 'a trembly time, not only with the Depression but with the Spanish Civil War and the Moscow Trials', but she remained sure that 'whatever the errors may turn out to have been, there was a great personal integrity to be found in the anti-Stalinist left, Trotskyite and others'.[54] MacNeice was generally less comfortable with such personal integrity that risked intolerance or intransigence. Both he and Clark, however, recognised the 'compassion' of many of those with whom she mixed. It was a word she later said 'has come to suggest crocodile tears, but in its proper meaning it's what moves us'.[55] MacNeice was fully aware of the 'proper meaning' of compassion, with its roots in the Latin 'com', 'with', and 'pati', 'to bear or suffer', as in the passion of Christ. But while this shared understanding allowed for a lively and sympathetic discussion of ideas it did not help them bridge the gap about the appropriate arenas for action.

Their friendship was distinguished by Clark asking MacNeice what he was doing or saying or writing to contribute to the betterment of society and MacNeice making the point that he was the one who had to decide what to do about the war, whether to be in it or out of it. For him, it was an all-encompassing question, but she was not at all sure a war to preserve the old systems was a constructive exercise. He would have chosen to remain in the States if she had agreed to marriage – he never quite got as far as actually proposing – but she was at best ambivalent. Ultimately, she was less interested in him than in what he stood for, and he was more interested in her than in what she stood for.

In 1944, Clark met Robert Penn Warren and married him in 1952. It was a marriage that would last. When America entered the war, Clark followed the example of MacNeice and committed to the effort, serving in the Office of Strategic Services – she was fluent in both French and Italian – setting aside her reservations as she had earlier challenged MacNeice to do. Years later, reflecting on a life that had seen her develop a reputation as a fine writer with a wry eye and close attention to detail, she observed apropos the challenge of being a 'woman' and a 'writer' that 'any time you get a big movement going, you'll get the lousy with the respectable, and the terms will get confused', and that 'if you're really busy doing something, you don't have time to go around complaining who prevented you from doing it'.[56] Clark came to be as distrustful of movements as was MacNeice. They had everything going for them except for the great gulf that existed for a few years between their two notions of what it actually meant to 'do' something.

Back in England and in the middle of a war, MacNeice got on with doing something, however ambivalently at times, and a stream of letters to Clark suddenly culminated with the news he had married again. MacNeice's new wife was Antoinette Millicent Hedley Anderson, known professionally and in her private life as Hedli. She was just a few months older than MacNeice and had established herself as a soprano singer, cabaret performer and actress with the Group Theatre after many years in Germany perfecting her craft and seeing early and at first hand the ravages brought about by Nazi ideology.[57] She returned home – she had been born in Surrey – via France and arrived in England as part of the wave of émigrés bringing the works of such people as Bertolt Brecht and Kurt Weil to the London stage. Auden wrote 'Four Cabaret Songs for Miss Hedli Anderson' for *The Ascent of F6*, written with Christopher Isherwood and performed by the Group Theatre in February and March 1937. Benjamin Britten wrote the music and Anderson appeared as the 'Cabaret Singer'. Later, one of its sections, 'Funeral Blues', would become widely known for its use in the 1994 film 'Four Weddings and a Funeral'. Anderson would also appear, with first billing, in a film that saw Peter Ustinov make his screen debut, the late 1940 documentary 'Hullo, Fame!' She had also worked for the GPO Film Unit and sang 'If you feel like expressing your affections' for a film introducing the British public to the new trunk dialling system and to the A and B buttons on public call boxes.

Anderson's career was prolific, she worked constantly and she was a significant presence in the same social circles as MacNeice. She knew Nancy Sharp well and brought an air of calm to what could be difficult gatherings, as William Coldstream observed when describing a party hosted by Britten and Anderson to see off Auden and Isherwood as they headed to New York in 1939:

> The evening was slightly sticky … The presence of two anti-boy women, Nancy and Inez [Spender], complicated the atmosphere because Benjamin [Britten] likes to be with Wystan & Christopher, all boys together without disturbing foreign elements such as slightly hostile ladies or gentlemen hostile to the gay music …
>
> Inez sat looking very self consciously composed – Nancy said Stephen took great pains to sit near her at regular intervals & occasionally touch her as a guarantee of stable affection when in the camp of the enemy … Hedli Anderson came in very theatrical and self assured. 'Queen of the boys tonight'. She really is very nice & very sane.[58]

It would be Anderson who started a relationship that moved beyond acquaintance to friendship to marriage, a marriage precipitated at least in part by the constraints of war and the difficulty she had accompanying MacNeice both to Belfast and to Éire. But by the time she and MacNeice married the big difference between that relationship and his others with Ezra, Sharp, and Clark was that Anderson's professional career was well and truly established, and she had no intention of becoming a traditional 1940s wife. Nor had MacNeice any intention of asking her to do so, but it meant that once the war ended the two of them were frequently in different places, she performing, he working on location for the BBC, and even when they were together one or the other was often chafing to be back doing the work each wanted. They would perform together at times, he reading his poetry and she singing. These joint tours could not compensate for the times when the two were separated, separation being especially difficult on Hedli, who would receive long letters from MacNeice expressing his love for her, his respect for her talents and a lengthy disquisition on how she might better employ her time for her own professional good.

He had, in 1942, just after their marriage, written a song cycle for her while they stayed in a cottage in County Down. As Anderson recalled

Our courtship was conducted to the strains of the *Pierrot Lunaire* cycle composed by Arnold Schoenberg to poems by Albert Giraud [which she was then performing in London]. Louis took a great dislike to the poetry … as set by Schoenberg and, shortly after our marriage … casually remarked that he would write a song-cycle for me … The first composer I approached with the cycle said he was no Schubert.[59]

Anderson never did perform the song cycle while MacNeice was alive, finally doing so as a spoken word piece in Cork, near where, in Scilly village, Kinsale, she then owned, operated and cooked in The Spinnaker restaurant, which became a haven for young Irish writers and artists in the 1970s. In retrospect, perhaps, it is telling that the song cycle begins

He went away,
The door fell to,
The sky was blue:
The sun shone easy,
The sun shone gay,
But he turned on his heel
And he went away.[60]

And though he does return, he does so dead from a war, and the singer is left to come to terms with the fact that

　you have betrayed me, you have deceived me,
You promised (me) you would return if I would wait;
I waited seven years for your returning
And you returned, yet you have deceived me.[61]

This sounds a lot like the lament Sylvie would have sung in *The Dark Tower* had there been a final, post-dragon reckoning back at Roland's family home.

Even at the beginning of the marriage MacNeice apparently saw in it the same potential for loss and abandonment that had marked his relations with his mother, his first wife, Sharp and Clark, and even, to an extent, with his sister, who remained always there, but always, too, a denizen of a life he considered just a little too dull and conventional. In the end, MacNeice and Anderson separated, and he started a relationship with the actress Mary Wimbush, whom he met at the BBC and with whom he bought the only house he would own, but his death two years later meant the course of that relationship was still undetermined.

Anderson, who used the name MacNeice from the day of her marriage until her death in 1990 in Paris, was as understanding of Louis as was his sister, and, like Elizabeth and Sharp, she guarded his reputation and explained him to others where he had himself been reckless with the first and uninterested in the second. Sharp and Anderson remained friends and, indeed, in 1991 Sharp exhibited a painting, 'Hedli MacNeice Enceinte.'[62] Three years earlier in Caen, France, Anderson had shared 'The Story of the House that Louis Built.'[63] It was 'a handsome house with thick walls'. Windows looked out on Connemara, on the Dorset Downs of his school years, on Iceland and on India. Where it was built she does not suggest, but, presumably, both London and Carrickfergus claimed its foundations. 'The front door was wide and always open' revealing an 'antechamber full of people coming and going' who would report Louis to be 'shy, arrogant, cold, polite, unapproachable'. Beyond that was a 'big Room with a Bar against which Louis would lean watching ... for the unexpected and the surprising'. And then came a room with 'shabby furniture ... books everywhere', a room where he was 'at ease, safe from the unexpected blow or the verbal knife in the back ... To these few people [admitted there] he gave all his affection and loyalty'. And past even this room was one with 'just space for two' with admittance reserved for the likes, one at a time, of Dylan Thomas or W.R. Rodgers, and only here would he 'discuss the making of poetry'. Beyond these rooms was a chamber where Louis could 'be alone with God, or as he called them the Great Presences, Greek or Roman, or again Dante, Spenser and the Elizabethans, and closer, to Yeats, Eliot and Auden.'[64]

'Upstairs there were two rooms'. One, nothing special, was where he 'received the casual lady encounter', but the other room was comfortable and smart, and there 'the five ladies of his life lingered', and linger they did, however long or short the actual relationship. There, said Hedli, could be found Mary Ezra, 'through [whom] he finally escaped from the Anglican church', and then four with 'worlds of their very own, a painter, a writer, a singer ... and a talented actress'.[65] And somewhere, unmentioned but watching fondly over all those rooms were his mother, who had loved Connemara, and his sister, who had understood him best.

NOTES

References to the poems of Louis MacNeice are as they appear in Peter McDonald (ed.), *Collected Poems* (London: Faber, 2007), except as noted.

1 Elizabeth Nicholson, 'Trees Were Green', in Terence Brown and Alec Reid (eds), *Time Was Away: The World of Louis MacNeice* (Dublin: Dolmen, 1974), pp.11–20 (p.11).
2 Louis MacNeice, 'Autobiography', pp.200–1.
3 'Autobiography', p.200; qtd in Nicholson, 'Trees', p.11.
4 Nicholson, 'Trees', p.11.
5 Ibid., pp.11–12.
6 Louis MacNeice, 'The Kingdom', VII, pp.247–8 (p.248).
7 Nicholson, 'Trees', p.12.
8 Ibid.
9 Ibid., p.13.
10 MacNeice, 'Autobiography', p.200.
11 The Tavistock and Portman NHS Foundation Trust, 'Our History, 1910s and 20s', <http://tavistockandportman.uk/sites/default/files/files/Our%20history_0.pdf>, accessed 22 July 2015.
12 J.S.R., 'Sir John Nicholson TD, MA, BM, BCH, FRCS', (obituary), *British Medical Journal*, 292 (29 March 1986), p.905.
13 Ian and Carole Dow, in conversation with the author. Summer 2003.
14 Geoffrey Grigson, *Recollections: Mainly of Writers and Artists* (London: Chatto and Windus, 1984), pp.72–6 (p.74).
15 Evelyn Waugh, *Brideshead Revisited, The Sacred & Profane Memories of Captain Charles Ryder* (London: Chapman and Hall, 1945).
16 Louis MacNeice, *The Poetry of W.B. Yeats* (Oxford: Oxford University Press, 1941), p.35.
17 Jon Stallworthy, *Louis MacNeice* (London: Faber, 1995), p.122.
18 Ibid., p.123.
19 E.R. Dodds, 'Louis MacNeice at Birmingham', in *Time Was Away*, pp.35–8 (p.36).
20 Ibid., p.36.
21 Louis MacNeice, *The Strings Are False: An Unfinished Autobiography*, ed. E.R. Dodds (London: Faber, 1965), p.150.
22 MacNeice, *Strings*, pp.150–1. The dating of the fire is from Stallworthy, *MacNeice*, p.171.
23 Ibid., p.151.
24 Ibid.
25 Surviving evidence indicates the only film Auden and Coldstream worked on together was 'Coal Face' (dir. Alberto Cavalcanti. London: GPO Film Unit, 1935). Auden wrote most of the narrative. Coldstream was the film editor, instrumental in helping implement 'the strategies adopted by the *documentary* movement … to explore the creative possibilities of filmmaking within the framework of such conventional narratives, and here this takes the form of a non-naturalistic deployment of sound, language and music, so that natural sounds, dialogue, speech, music and choral singing are integrated in a dramatic, often

strident manner' [Ian Aitken, 'Coal Face', BFI Screen Online, <http://www.screenonline. org.uk/film/id/461606/>, accessed 24 July 2015].

26 Philip Spender, 'Introduction', in *Nancy Sharp (Nancy Spender), 1909–2001 Memorial Exhibition: Paintings & Works on Paper* (London: The Estate of Nancy Spender, 2002), np.

27 Ibid.

28 Anthony Powell, *The Acceptance World*, Vol. 3 of *A Dance to the Music of Time* (London: Mandarin, 1991), p.49.

29 Kathleen Bell, 'Nancy Spender's Recollections of Wystan Auden', *W.H. Auden Society Newsletter*, 10 and 11 (September 1993), pp.1–3 (p.1).

30 Stallworthy, *MacNeice*, p.203.

31 'Nancy Spender', (obituary), *The Daily Telegraph*, 27 June 2001, <http://www.telegraph. co.uk/news/obituaries/1310454/Nancy-Spender.html>, accessed 24 July 2015. The biblical reference is to Isaiah 44:16.

32 Stallworthy, *MacNeice*, p.203.

33 Spender, 'Introduction', np.

34 '"A Gift of Autumn": Nancy Spender in Conversation with Jon Stallworthy', prod. Piers Plowright. London: BBC Radio 3, Friday 2 November 1990.

35 Spender, 'Introduction', np.

36 Ibid. Sharp's portrait of MacNeice now hangs in the National Portrait Gallery (NPG 6628) <http://www.npg.org.uk/collections/search/portrait/mw11412/Frederick-Louis-MacNeice? LinkID=mp09538&role=sit&rNo=0>. Sharp had offered it to the National Portrait Gallery soon after the death of MacNeice, but it was rejected on the grounds that both the sitter and the artist were 'adulterers' at the time of the painting. Details of the rejection were provided to me while in conversation with Barney and Dinora Davies-Rees, who bought Sir John and Lady Elizabeth Nicholson's house after their deaths and treated me with great kindness and generosity whenever I had occasion to visit. Dinora was the stepdaughter of David Bomberg.

37 Stallworthy, *MacNeice*, p.226.

38 John Sutherland, *Stephen Spender: A Literary Life* (Oxford: Oxford University Press, 2005), p.280

39 Ibid.

40 Philip Spender, personal correspondence [email], 1 September 2015. The various dates and details throughout this paragraph were provided or confirmed by Spender.

41 Robert Medley interviewed by Andrew Lambirth, 'National Life Stories: Artists' Lives' (London: The British Library), p.184 C466/19/02 F4109 Side A, <http://sounds.bl.uk/related-content/TRANSCRIPTS/021T-C0466X0019XX-ZZZZA0.pdf>, accessed 10 August 2015.

42 The Royal Geographical Society, 'Michael Spender', Imaging Everest, <http:// imagingeverest.rgs.org/Units/73.html>, accessed 24 July 2015.

43 John Margetson, 'Nancy Spender', (obituary), *The Guardian*, 25 June 2001, <http://www. theguardian.com/news/2001/jun/25/guardianobituaries.arts>, accessed 24 July 2015.

44 Peter Freeth, 'Nancy Spender at the Camden Institute', in *Nancy Sharp (Nancy Spender), 1909–2001 Memorial Exhibition*, np.

45 Ibid.

46 Nancy Sharp [Coldstream] to John Auden, 15 September 1939. The letter, which is in private hands, is dated 15 September but was obviously composed over several days. One

shilling and 3 pence was the equivalent of 15ᵈ, so the cost of an airmail letter to India had increased by 900 per cent between 1 September and the date this letter was mailed sometime in the second half of September.

47 Margetson, 'Nancy Spender'. The school later merged with another to become the Archbishop Michael Ramsey School.

48 Sally Hunter; qtd in Margetson, 'Nancy Spender'.

49 [Colton Johnson], 'Eleanor Clark', Vassar Encyclopedia, Distinguished Alumnae/i, <https://vcencyclopedia.vassar.edu/alumni/eleanor-clark.html>, accessed 27 July 2015.

50 'Four Members of News Board to Start Magazine', *The Vassar Miscellany News*, XVI:47 (25 May 1932), p.1; qtd in Gary Fountain and Peter Brazeau, *Remembering Elizabeth Bishop: An Oral Biography* (Amherst, MA: University of Massachusetts Press, 1994), p.362n.

51 Bethany Hicok, 'Elizabeth Bishop's "Queer Birds": Vassar, "Con Spirito", and the Romance of Female Community', *Contemporary Literature*, 40:2 (summer, 1999), pp.286–310 (p.286).

52 Clark is usually identified as a member of the board, but she later said she 'had nothing to do with it', having left Vassar in 1933 to study at Barnard College for a year. Frances Kiernan, *Seeing Mary Plain: A Life of Mary McCarthy* (New York, NY: Norton, 2000), p.80.

53 Stallworthy, *MacNeice*, p.183.

54 R.W.B. Lewis, 'Talk with Eleanor Clark', *The New York Times Book Review*, 16 October 1977, pp.11, 40–1 (p.40).

55 Ibid., p.40.

56 'Interview with Eleanor Clark and Robert Penn Warren', *New England Review*, 1 (1978) pp.49–70; repr. in Gloria L. Cronin and Ben Siegel (eds), *Conversations with Robert Penn Warren* (Jackson, MS: University Press of Mississippi, 2005), pp.150–64 (p.157).

57 For more details of this part of her life, see Katherine Firth, '"Queen of the Boys Tonight": Hedli Anderson and the "Auden Gang"', Louis MacNeice Centenary Conference and Celebration, Queen's University, Belfast, September 2007, <https://www.academia.edu/3984288/Queen_of_the_boys_tonight_Hedli_Anderson_and_the_Auden_Gang_Katherine_Firth>, accessed 19 October 2014.

58 Benjamin Britten, *Letters from a Life: The Selected Letters and Diaries of Benjamin Britten 1913-1976* Vol 2, *1939-45*, ed. Donald Mitchell and Philip Reed (London: Faber, 1991), p.548. It should be noted here that 'boy' and 'anti-boy' are simply the code preferred by Auden, Isherwood and co. for admitted homosexuality and associated cultural preferences, or objection thereto.

59 Hedli MacNeice, 'Introduction', in Louis MacNeice, *The Revenant: A Song-Cycle for Hedli Anderson* (Dublin: Cuala, 1975), pp.7–8 (p.7).

60 MacNeice, 'The Revenant', I, p.9.

61 Ibid., XI, p.28.

62 Nancy Sharp, 'Hedli MacNeice Enceinte', oil on canvas, 41cm by 51cm and 'clearly unfinished'. Private collection.

63 Hedli MacNeice, 'The Story of the House that Louis Built', in Jacqueline Genet and Wynne Hellegouarc'h (eds), *Studies on Louis MacNeice* (Caen: Centre de Publications de l'Université de Caen, 1988), pp.9–10.

64 Ibid., pp.8–9.

65 Ibid., p.9.

CHAPTER 5

The Early Works

Louis MacNeice grew up in a household full of words, almost all of them weighted with meaning. His father's sermons were about two lives: the one lived now on earth, temporal and immediate, and the one lived eternally, timeless and intimated. There were fairy stories, with their dual layer of action and moral. But there was on occasion something more lighthearted; 'impressive and awe-inspiring' though the rector was, he 'had too much warmth and evident humanity to be really frightening'.[1] He was a man not afraid to make his opinion clear on even seemingly small matters, as when he considered the appropriate care of cemeteries: 'artificial flowers under glass covers are much to be deprecated. They display a deplorable lack of taste'.[2] He could 'produce quite respectable doggerel verse on any given subject, and would occasionally carry on a rhyming correspondence with various friends'.[3]

MacNeice wrote some poetry before starting at Marlborough in September 1921 and continued to do so throughout his school years. In the pseudonymous novel, *Roundabout Way*, Devlin Urquhart, MacNeice's near alter ego, responds to the question whether he used 'ever to rant poetry [at school] … I don't mean recite it [but] rant it' with the abrupt acknowledgment, 'Of course I did. I used to do it all over'.[4] He would continue to write at Merton College, Oxford – he went up in 1926 – and his first collection, *Blind Fireworks*, appeared in 1929, published by Victor Gollancz. This was followed by *Roundabout Way* in 1932 and then, in 1935, by the volume that began to cement his reputation, *Poems*, published by T.S. Eliot at Faber.[5]

Blind Fireworks offers only the occasional glimpse of the insight MacNeice would take from poets such as Eliot, for whom a 'thought … is, in most cases, really an experience of the first value'.[6] The failure of several newer poets to recognise this, William Empson in particular, resulted in poems in which 'thoughts rank far below sensations … frigid intellectual exercises (though very good practice for undergraduates)'.[7]

Some of the poems in *Blind Fireworks* are themselves little more than an 'intellectual exercise', but suggestions of what would be a recurrent trope throughout MacNeice's work – the connections between thought and experience, the personal and the universal, the past and the present – are apparent in poems such as 'Reminiscences of Infancy', with its memory of trains that ran past the rectory in Carrickfergus 'Sliding downhill gently to the bottom of the distance | (For now all things are there that all were here once)'.[8] From the start, MacNeice was attentive to the tension between life's expectations and its demands, to the dread that creeps in upon consciousness. 'The whole of life – the interim'[9] should remind us not to

> put too much on the sympathy of things,
> The dregs of drink, the dried cups of flowers,
> The pathetic fallacy of the passing hours
> When it is we who pass them.[10]

Introducing *New Signatures* in 1932, Michael Roberts, the pseudonym of William Edward Roberts, identified an 'impersonality' in MacNeice 'nearer the Greek conception of good citizenship than to the stoical austerity of recent verse'.[11] For the double-first Oxford classics scholar, 'good citizenship' was not so much impersonal as it was an ideal and a practical guide. But MacNeice had learned, too, from Pythagoras and would later stipulate that while 'your unconscious and your opinions are both important … neither is the main concern of … poetry; poetry lies between, though not cut off from either. Poetry consists in a ratio'.[12] MacNeice later judged that *Blind Fireworks* never quite got the ratio right, but when he acknowledged the need 'to ask, though I fear I'll get no answer – | "What is the answer to your riddle?"'[13] he already knew that questions, not answers, are at the heart of composing a life of meaning.

After *Blind Fireworks* was published, MacNeice secured a position as an assistant lecturer in classics at Birmingham University. His head of department would be E.R. Dodds, a fellow Ulsterman with whom MacNeice developed a close relationship. Dodds had got to know W.B. Yeats and AE (George Russell) in Dublin in the years before partition and remained a Nationalist throughout his life. The friendship with Dodds offered MacNeice a connection to another aspect of Ireland and Irish identity that complemented his father's and stepmother's worlds, and it helped to secure him an introduction to meet Yeats in Rathfarnham in 1934.

His major creative focus turned toward the only novel he would complete and see through to publication, *Roundabout Way*. In an odd coincidence, he selected as the surname for the pseudonymous author, Louis Malone, the road on which his father would live as Bishop of Down and Connor and Dromore.[14]

Roundabout Way was published in London and New York by Putnam's in 1932. *The Spectator* noted it as a tale of the 'modern generation when it comes down from Oxford, with very few jobs, but plenty to do'.[15] It was also a book about which its author would later say he had been 'disloyal to myself [and] wrote a novel which purported to be an idyll of domestic felicity'.[16] This fails to recognise that *Roundabout Way* was his second novel – the first might have been called 'Your Esteemed Order' – and that he would work on two other novels for several years, 'The Family Vet' and 'Going Out and Coming In', both ultimately abandoned. MacNeice might also have been at work in this period on an idea from his undergraduate days, 'A Baedeker's Guide to Purgatory'.

Roundabout Way was a paean to his recent marriage to Mary Ezra, or, at least, an indication of his sentiments about how he ought to feel about marriage. Yet not that long before his own marriage, MacNeice had returned

to Ireland for my sister Elizabeth's wedding. I felt guilty because I had no strong feelings on the subject … That evening one of the bridesmaids and I took one of Elizabeth's wedding presents, a huge and hideous china jar – the sort of thing you put a palm in – and rolled it downstairs to smash at the feet of my step-mother. Full stop. Exclamation mark. Anyone who got married – so I felt – had left the world on a tangent.

Back in Oxford I was more than usually lonely.[17]

In Birmingham, MacNeice settled into establishing himself as a lecturer, working on a study of Latin humour with which he continued to tinker for many years. He began engaging in the social life of the faculty while embracing his and his wife's idea of what marriage should entail. For a while the combination worked. MacNeice reported to one friend that 'we have just been planting our five roses', which he identified by their various English varietal names, before adding that their maid's 'cakes are wonderful; Mary makes them, too, with full artistry. We are eating one at the moment.'[18] He must have been writing some poetry because in April 1932 he was in touch with Eliot at Faber, who recognised promise but not yet the makings of a volume. Encouraged, MacNeice began to shape the poems that would form the basis of *Poems*, which Faber would publish in 1935. They took the opportunity of his volume being less immediately 'political' than much new poetry to describe the author as 'the most original Irish poet of his generation, dour without sentimentality, intensely serious without political enthusiasm.'[19] This resoundingly backhanded set of compliments also indicates a distinctly London-centric view of 'Irish' poetry.

The collection opens with an 'Eclogue for Christmas'. MacNeice trusted his readers to identify the tension between the traditional meaning of the word in English, that of a pastoral poem, and the reference to Virgil's *Eclogae*, a word that can comfortably be rendered in English as 'reckonings'. 'I meet you in an evil time', the poem and book begin.[20] It is a compelling invocation for the son of a bishop and an advocate of individual moral choice, especially set against the promise of Christmas.

The response to that opening line – 'The evil bells | Put out of our heads, I think, the thought of everything else'[21] – is at the heart of claims MacNeice would make throughout his poetry. While the speakers' joint conclusion is that 'We shall go down like palaeolithic man | Before some new Ice Age or Genghiz Khan,'[22] they take comfort in the conscious celebration of the connection between the human and the natural:

> And on the bare and high
> Places of England, the Wiltshire Downs and the Long Mynd
> Let the balls of my feet bounce on the turf, my face burn in the wind
> My eyelashes stinging in the wind, and the sheep like grey stones
> Humble my human pretensions –
> ....

> Let all these so ephemeral things
> Be somehow permanent like the swallow's tangent wings.[23]

Such yearnings in the face of broader tensions found MacNeice also questioning his relationship with Ireland. His attitude would evolve, but in *Poems* his valediction to the country of his parents is determined, sure that 'what you have given me [is] | Indifference and sentimentality'.[24] He remembers the boxes of stationery his father had in his office, with their 'trade-mark of a hound and a round tower, | And that was Irish glamour',[25] such glamour off-set by 'each new fantasy of badge and gun'.[26] Aware that otherwise he had 'to gesture, | Take part in, or renounce, each imposture', MacNeice determines to 'resign', to say farewell to the 'chequered and the quiet hills | The gaudily striped Atlantic', to the 'greyhounds and your hunters beautifully bred | Your drums and your dolled-up Virgins and your ignorant dead'.[27] Yet only two or three years later he would refer unironically to the 'lost six counties of the Emerald Isle'.[28]

To some extent this was easy posturing. MacNeice was making his new life and whatever was happening in Ireland, or had happened, was no longer personal. Poetry was. He found models in Eliot's careful constructions and also in the work of the First World War poets such as Wilfred Owen, for whom 'The poetry is in the pity'.[29] Owen 'grew up in readiness to write like Keats', but the war 'dissolved the Keats' in him and hence the self-pity.[30] MacNeice criticised those poets of whom he said,

> All you do is hedge
> And shirk the inevitable issue, all you do
> Is shear your sheep to stop your ears.
> Poetry you think is only the surface vanity,
> The painted nails, the hips narrowed by fashion,
> The hooks and eyes of words; but it is not that only.[31]

The pity of all humans, which poets who wish to be honest must record, 'is to be mortal | And with Here and Now for your anvil'.[32] The irony of this defence is that it is delivered by Death, the interlocutor of the two shepherds standing in for poets in homage to the tradition of the eclogue. It was fitting, then, that *Poems* could end with the 'Ode' written to welcome the poet's son, Dan, into the world. It was the father's hope that the son might learn to 'ride two horses at once, a foot on each',[33] without 'halving the truth' or being 'caught between jagged edges'.[34] Dan, he hoped, might find the synthesis between the immediate and the eternal. For all his attention to the privilege and panic of mortality, MacNeice could not

> draw up any code
> There are too many qualifications
> Too many asterisk asides
> Too many crosses in the margin
> But as others, forgetting the others,
> Run after the nostrums
> Of science art and religion
> So would I mystic and maudlin
> Dream of the both real and ideal.[35]

'Ode' was also a response-of-sorts to Yeats, who, MacNeice would later point out, was 'a very single-minded or whole-minded artist. Take hints if you like but for God's sake don't imitate him'.[36] He was talking about Yeats's dramas, but 'Ode' finds MacNeice following his own advice, offering his 'no thanks' to Yeats, delivered as a re-envisioning of the older poet's 'A Prayer for my Daughter'.[37]

Writing in *The Spectator*, Ian Parsons drew attention to the collection's strength and distinctiveness: 'The first thing one notices about these thirty poems ... is that they are totally un-didactic', which set MacNeice apart from 'the group of which Mr Auden is the acknowledged leader'.[38] In the stronger poems,

> Fragments of experience ... are combined to form an imaginative whole. And it is significant ... that [MacNeice] should find this unity in himself, in a personal equation, rather than in any political doctrine or established creed. For the danger to the artist in all formalised systems of belief is that they flatter the intellect at the expense of the heart, and that intuitions which may start as perfectly genuine emotional responses end nearly always as the coldest of rationalisations. It is then a short step from art which is also good propaganda to propaganda that is very bad art.[39]

The volume also caused Yeats to re-think his earlier evaluation of MacNeice, and in the introduction to the 1936 *Oxford Book of Modern*

Verse Yeats described MacNeice and his contemporaries by observing that 'after the war certain poets combined the modern vocabulary, the accurate record of the relevant facts learned from Eliot, with the sense of suffering of the war poets … [Cecil] Day Lewis, [Charles] Madge, MacNeice, are modern through the character of their intellectual passion.'[40] Yeats identified MacNeice as an 'anti-communist [who] … contemplates the modern world with even greater horror than the communist Day Lewis', no more accurate a description of MacNeice than his effort a year earlier – Yeats enjoyed defining things and people and places; MacNeice preferred to complicate them. Yeats included more of MacNeice's poems than he did of either Auden or Stephen Spender.[41]

Poems concluded with the 'Ode' to his new son and was dedicated, 'to my wife', but almost immediately after the volume appeared Mary left MacNeice and Dan for America and life with Charles Katzman, whom they had been hosting. Suddenly, the poet who had regretted that 'we are obsolete who like the lesser things'[42] now had to re-make the life he had perhaps too precipitously decided could be patterned out of an ideal of domestic bliss. The passing hours now passed more slowly, and MacNeice came out of his early-adulthood idyll to find that in 'England one forgets'

there is no room to stoop
And look along the ground, one cannot see the ground
For the feet of the crowd, and the lost is never found.
I dropped something, I think, but I am not sure what
And cannot say if it mattered much or not.[43]

Perhaps in part relieved by the end of a marriage they had never fully embraced, MacNeice's father, stepmother and sister would regularly step into the breach over the next few years, taking in Dan and his nurse whenever MacNeice took to the road to pay some bills. MacNeice spent August and September 1936 in Iceland at the invitation of Auden, whom he had known for some years but had become closer to after the move to Birmingham introduced him to Auden's father, the public health doctor for the city and a lecturer at the university. As MacNeice's respect for Auden's poetry grew and his doubts about Anthony Blunt's ability to move beyond doctrinaire adherence to communism strengthened, the Iceland trip cemented what would remain an important relationship.

In Iceland, news from the rest of Europe was sparse, but in the stories of the sagas, with which both poets had been familiar since school, and in a landscape redolent with mythic overtones and geological foreboding, they found plenty of opportunity to consider the relationship between civilisation and the individual. *Letters from Iceland* is a peculiar book, a hotchpotch of entries, most written individually by either Auden or MacNeice and almost none about Iceland except for some selective reprinting of material from previous accounts of the island. Among MacNeice's contributions is a letter to Blunt constructed around the conceit that those involved are schoolgirls. MacNeice is Hetty, Blunt is Nancy and Auden is Maisie. It is a letter which reveals MacNeice's eye for detail and domestic gossip, as when he describes a stop during the horseback crossing of central Iceland. The cabin was

deplorably cold and the wooden platform … hard under my sleeping-bag. I thought very hard and managed to remember a Latin quotation – probitas laudatus et alget – which means roughly that it is a fine thing to be a Girl Guide but that you can't keep warm in kudos. How only too true, darling. 'Never again' Maisie and I have been saying to each other.[44]

Auden was consistent in stating his preference for an urban and industrial landscape and, as the party prepared to depart, 'Hetty' reflected:

I mean, *I mean, darling*, does one come to Iceland for this? It's all very well for Maisie; it's copy for her … but when this pack of girls gets in The Great Open Spaces goodness knows what is going to happen. Sprained ankles is the least I should think … Talking of the G.O. Spaces Maisie says they are a closed book. I have been wondering if this would be considered an epigram because I couldn't see that it was very funny and Maisie is supposed to be witty, but then it is different in London, where people have been drinking sherry before you say anything to them.[45]

Such humour had also lightened the plot of a play MacNeice wrote for the Group Theatre while in Birmingham but which the Group rejected. 'Station Bell' was about the rise of an Irish dictator, Julia Brown. The Birmingham University Dramatic Society performed the play, apparently in something of a rush, in early 1937. The reviewer noted 'slapstick, satire and moments of real tension' in that order, albeit that the production was marred by an 'uncertainty that amounted to somnambulism'.[46] Exactly what, if any, input MacNeice had in the production is unclear, but the cast included the future poet and BBC dramatist Henry Reed, 'in a part that contained much wry smiling'.[47] The production also contained a 'mad clergyman … [with] a true fanatical gleam'.[48] Both the habit of smiling wryly and concern about the dangers of fanaticism, religious or secular, would remain distinguishing tropes of MacNeice's work.

Back in London after the Iceland trip, MacNeice started teaching at Bedford College and in October Faber published *The Agamemnon of Aeschylus,* which he had finished translating in Birmingham and which the Group Theatre would produce in November. Rupert Doone directed the work, about which he had 'initially been unenthusiastic', given what he perceived as its distance from contemporary commentary, which was the troupe's *raison d'être*.[49] The music was written by Benjamin Britten, to whom MacNeice had been introduced by Auden and who had also been responsible for bringing MacNeice to the attention of Doone. MacNeice advocated a production that should 'tend toward the statuesque' and be 'rather larger-than-life', albeit that he was not clear about how these two goals might be achieved on stage.[50] His suggested direction was further confusing in that he requested 'classical Greek dress … be avoided' but wanted the dress to contain 'hints from the Mycenean age'.[51] In an attempt to help audiences perceive a connection to contemporary matters, Doone had Aegisthus's 'soldiers offering a Nazi salute',[52] but, otherwise, the scenery and costumes were a mishmash of ideas and the 'production [notes] … make often hilarious reading'.[53] This unintended comedy was unavoidable, for MacNeice, however determined to be modern, was a staunch advocate of the value of the original, as one review observed:

> MacNeice's work is described on the dust-cover as the first 'contemporary' translation of the play by a poet, and if 'contemporary' means modern, it is at first sight modern enough … But under this modern covering further inspection reveals a translation unusually faithful and honest.[54]

In 1937, in-between lecturing and his travels, MacNeice completed his second original drama, *Out of the Picture*. It would be published by Faber and staged, in a heavily adapted form, by the Group Theatre. *Out of the Picture* aggressively questions the degree to which personal identity and resolve matter in a society that has itself lost a sense of purpose. The play opens in a bare room with a radio announcing the resumption of a peace conference aimed at 'preventing the outbreak of war'.[55] The commentary summarising its likelihood of success is turned off at the point the announcer declares the obstacles to success to be 'if not insurmountable, at least –'.[56] Throughout the play, that refrain will recur between acts and within acts. The personal lives playing out on stage are ultimately unresolved and perhaps unresolvable in the midst of the news from abroad. In an unintended indication of where his interests, and work, would soon turn, MacNeice personalises the medium of radio, introducing Listener-In and Radio-Announcer, who appear on stage between scenes to offer a play within a play that just might be a celebration of the immediacy of radio.

At the same time as he had been finishing *Out of the Picture* MacNeice had been at work on his next travelogue, a trip to the Hebrides. The resulting book, *I Crossed the Minch*, found him assessing his life. He was about to turn 30 and thinking it time to outgrow his adolescence and address the fact that 'Most good poems … are a collaboration between Jekyll and Hyde. With me it is mostly Hyde – self-pity, greed, nostalgia.'[57] Both Jekyll and Hyde had informed *Out of the Picture*, but, unlike in Stephenson's novella itself,[58] there was finally no real connection between the two parts of the drama and the play ends up a largely formless series of scenes rushing toward an absurdist conclusion. The radio interjections, however, do create something of a cohesive whole, reaching a denouement when Radio-Announcer interrupts his regularly scheduled programming to ask Listener-In for a moment of his time in light of concern that 'the wireless is going to be appropriated for military purposes. Its function in future will be not pleasure but utility.'[59]

Important though utility might be, Listener-In also values pleasure and is 'sorry' for the information.[60] Not long after, Listener-In decides he can no longer stomach the news, refuses to adjust the dial, stops listening and leaves Radio-Announcer disconsolate with the realisation 'No listeners, no radio.'[61] Listener-In then takes up the challenge of filling the dead air he has created, offering a hymn to the personal in the midst of uncertainty, a hymn that would find full expression in a book-length poem two years later:

My talk this evening is entitled 'Summer is A-Comen In'.[62]
You needn't listen if you don't want to.
Summer is a-Comen in. Soon we must change the clocks,
Give up our coal fire, fill the grate with lilac.

....

But will this summer run true to type?
The official announcers would never mention them
But there are certain factors to be considered.
First, there is a war about to be declared.
Second – but who cares about the second?[63]

There was no denying 'Things are not what they were, the time is past |
For growing in a quiet plot | For sleeping in an easy bed.'[64]

I Crossed the Minch is also a book in some sense 'all very out of order',
a partial recounting of MacNeice's travels on a few Hebridean islands.
It has the charming distinction of its author admitting he is writing for
the money and has not given a lot of thought to his audience, except to
assume that people who like this sort of book will like this sort of book.
The book is part travelogue and part memoir, and it offers MacNeice the
opportunity to reflect on his life to date. As he travelled toward the islands,
he recalled the transition when headed 'west and south' in Ireland, 'from
degraded Ulster with its brooks running from the factories sulphur-yellow,
stinking of chlorine, and its faces stiff with the fear of giving a point to
anyone'.[65] He expected something similar as he put London behind him,
to whose cultural circles he had automatic admission by virtue of family
and education but which he found at times almost surreal, a place where
'people keep asking one for lifts to Finsbury Park or to dramatise *Wuthering
Heights*'.[66]

Among the conceits of *I Crossed the Minch* are occasional dialogues
between various 'participants' on the journey that echo the eclogues of
Poems and some of the tone of *Out of the Picture*. Several are overheard
conversations between Perceval and Crowder, imagined commentators
on MacNeice's psyche and motivations. The longest dialogue is that
between MacNeice and his Guardian Angel. The angel asks if MacNeice
has read

　　　　　that nice book by your friend Spender ...
ME:　　*Forward from Liberalism.*

G.A.:   That's it ... that reminds me – speaking in my professional
         capacity, don't you think it's almost time *you* had an attitude
         to these subjects?

ME: Why? ... You think the world would be the least little teeny
         bit interested? Besides I can't tell the world what I think
         before I've thought it.[67]

MacNeice was reticent about any public statement, suspecting it
would be no different than the reason 'a great many people go to a play as
they might go up Snowdon or visit the Giant's Causeway, in order to say
they have been there'.[68] People went to church or took up causes for the
same reason, and perhaps even went to his beloved international rugby
matches in that spirit, albeit that he suggested the highpoint of drama had
been fifth century BCE Athens where plays were 'produced ... on only two
occasions during the year [so] they were therefore an event to be waited
for, like the Calcutta Cup'.[69]

MacNeice was accompanied for some of his travels by the woman with
whom he was having an affair, Nancy Sharp, then married to the painter
William Coldstream. Sharp, who was introduced when in the Hebrides as
MacNeice's wife in order to avoid the complications that would result from
admitting any other relationship, provided eight illustrations but is not
mentioned once in the book itself. She would also provide the illustrations
for the delightfully haphazard guide to London Zoo that appeared in late
1938 as, simply, *Zoo*.[70]

If MacNeice had been working his way toward the task of bearing
private witness to public events, his next collection, *The Earth Compels*,
made clear the extent to which his poetry had grown toward satisfying that
intention. Dedicated 'to Nancy', the collection opens with 'Carrickfergus',
grounding the volume in a very specific sense of place and origin, both
spatial and temporal. This was First World War Carrickfergus, where
MacNeice had thought that 'never again || Would the weekly papers not
have photos of sandbags | And my governess not make bandages from
moss'.[71] As such worries returned once more to Britain, the relationship
with Sharp was more vital by the day. Yet that relationship had reached a
critical and complicated point, with her husband even going so far as to
suggest the three of them live together with their three children. So while
'Carrickfergus' looked back, the next poem, 'June Thunder', recorded a
summer 'downpour | Breaking the blossoms of our overdated fancies | Our

old sentimentality and whimsicality'.[72] The immediate effect of this 'cleansing' was the recognition of the return of loneliness and the admission that 'If only now you would come I should be happy | Now if now only'.[73]

It was precisely the momentary nature of any possibly remaining joy that made it all the more important, for

> Our freedom as free lances
> Advances towards its end;
> The earth compels, upon it
> Sonnets and birds descend;
> And soon, my friend,
> We shall have no time for dances.[74]

MacNeice came from an island and the previous two summers he had spent time on islands, but, as he had learned in Iceland, the news from the mainland called, and

> Minute your gesture but it must be made –
> Your hazard, your act of defiance and hymn of hate,
> Hatred of hatred, assertion of human values,
> Which is now your only duty.
> ....
> And, it may be added, it is your only chance.[75]

MacNeice's relationship with Sharp was his gesture, his assertion of the personal in the face of the political. It was a relationship that resulted in some of the great love poetry of the twentieth century. Leaving Barra at the end of his second trip to the Hebrides, MacNeice wished for Sharp's company, who stood 'for so much that I wish for', who offered 'the example | Of living like a fugue and moving' and who was 'alive beyond question'.[76] This was what the times demanded, a determination to keep moving and to celebrate the human, and so he recorded his return to Ireland for the 12 February 1938 Five Nations match against England, travelling to Lansdowne Road and finding that 'what was jaded' now 'rejoiced'.[77] He skirted over the final score, Ireland 14–36 England, reporting only 'Eccentric scoring – Nicholson, Marshall and Unwin | Replies by Bailey and Daly',[78] although that would seem to have been poetic licence as of those named only Mike Marshall, one of the

England locks, was neither a wing nor a centre. What eccentricity in scoring there was might have been that both sides scored 14 points in the final ten minutes of the match.

The Earth Compels celebrated those who could enjoy a rugby match and who, like Sharp, had

> felt the death-wish too,
> But your lust for life prevails –
> Drinking coffee, telling tales.
>
> Our prerogatives as men
> Will be cancelled who knows when;
> Still I drink your health before
> The gun-butt raps upon the door.[79]

MacNeice looked for his comfort in the human kindnesses of the day-to-day, believing in the importance of the moment, distrusting history or politics as validating agencies. 'My chief pleasures … are liking and being liked',[80] he had noted earlier, yet he had learned from his father that the day-to-day is fleeting. In Iceland and the Hebrides he had had time to reflect after the loss of marriage and the growth of a new love, and as Europe tumbled toward another war he took comfort that there are those 'Whose common sense or sense of humour or mere | Desire for self-assertion won them through',[81] but even these victories were fleeting, for they won through

> not to happiness. Though at intervals
> They paused in sunlight for a moment's fusion
> With friends or nature till the cynical wind
> Blew the trees pale –.[82]

'Believing man responsible for what he does | Sole author of his terror and his content' and so 'The duty his to learn',[83] MacNeice delivered with *The Earth Compels* as full a demonstration as was possible that he had done his duty and had learned what needed to be learned. What followed was a poem genuinely deserving of the word epic, for the heroic was in the ordinary, a poem in which 'apprehensiveness [has rarely] sounded more human or humanity so worth preserving'.[84]

NOTES

References to the poems of Louis MacNeice are as they appear in Peter McDonald (ed.), *Collected Poems* (London: Faber, 2007), except as noted.

1. John Hilton, 'Louis MacNeice at Marlborough and Oxford' in Louis MacNeice, *The Strings Are False: An Unfinished Autobiography*, ed. E.R. Dodds (London: Faber, 1965), pp.239–84 (p.255).

2   [John Frederick MacNeice], 'The Care of Churchyards', in *United Diocese of Down and Connor and Dromore Year Book 1937* (Glasgow: Ecclesiastical Press, [1937]), np.

3   Elizabeth Nicholson, 'Trees Were Green' in Terence Brown and Alec Reid (eds), *Time Was Away: The World of Louis MacNeice* (Dublin: Dolmen, 1974), pp.11–20 (p.15).

4   Louis Malone [Louis MacNeice], *Roundabout Way* (London: Putnam's, 1932); reprinted as *'Roundabout Way' by Louis MacNeice* (London: Capuchin Classics, 2012), p.134.

5   For a bibliography of MacNeice's works and for some works about him, see C.M. Armitage and Neil Clark, *A Bibliography of the Works of Louis MacNeice* (Edmonton: University of Alberta Press, 1973), although there are errors and omissions in this work; see also Alan Heuser, 'Bibliography of Short Prose by Louis MacNeice (Corrected)', in *Selected Prose of Louis MacNeice*, ed. Alan Heuser (Oxford: Clarendon, 1990), pp.275–92.

6   Louis MacNeice, 'Poetry To-day' in Geoffrey Grigson (ed.), *The Arts Today* (London: John Lane, 1935), pp.25–67 (p.23); repr. in Alan Heuser (ed.), *Selected Literary Criticism of Louis MacNeice* (Oxford: Clarendon, 1987), pp.10–44. MacNeice is picking up on Eliot's argument in, T.S. Eliot, 'The Metaphysical Poets', rev. of *Metaphysical Lyrics and Poems of the Seventeenth Century: Donne to Butler. Selected and Edited, with an Essay by Herbert J.C. Grierson* (Oxford: Clarendon, 1921), *Times Literary Supplement*, 1031 (20 October 1921), pp.669–70. 'Poetry To-day' formed the basis of the 1938 study *Modern Poetry* (London: Oxford University Press).

7   Ibid., p.23.

8   Louis MacNeice, 'Reminiscences of Infancy', p.615.

9   Louis MacNeice, 'Cradle Song for Miriam', pp.659–60 (p.660).

10 Louis MacNeice, 'Mayfly', pp.31–2 (p.32).

11 Michael Roberts, 'Preface', *New Signatures: Poems by Several Hands*, Hogarth Living Poets 24 (London: Hogarth, 1932), pp.7–20; qtd. in MacNeice, 'Poetry To-day', p.11.

12 MacNeice, 'Poetry To-day', pp.36–7.

13 Louis MacNeice, 'Fire and Coal', pp.633–4 (p.634).

14 Now called MacNeice House, the building at 77 Malone Road is the home of the Arts Council of Northern Ireland. It was purchased by the diocese in 1935 and was sold soon after MacNeice's death. In a further twist of fate, the house had been built for Denis Johnston's grandfather and Johnston had spent time there as a young boy, just as MacNeice's son, Dan, would spend time there early in his life.

15 'Further Fiction' [including a brief notice of Louis Malone, *Roundabout Way* (London: Putnam, 1932)], *The Spectator*, 5448 (25 November 1932), p.30.

16 The Poetry Foundation, 'Louis MacNeice', <http://www.poetryfoundation.org/bio/louis-macneice>, accessed 13 October 2014.

17 Louis MacNeice, *The Strings Are False: An Unfinished Autobiography*, ed. E.R. Dodds (London: Faber, 1965), p.118.

18 Louis MacNeice to John Hilton, p.227.

19 Louis MacNeice, *Poems* (London: Faber, 1935), dust jacket blurb.

20 Louis MacNeice, 'An Eclogue for Christmas', pp.3–7 (p.3).

21 Ibid.

22 Ibid., p.4.

23 Ibid., p.7. The Wiltshire Downs are where he went to school and the Long Mynd is a heathland plateau in the Shropshire hills, where the MacNeices visited on several occasions after settling in Birmingham.

24 Louis MacNeice, 'Valediction', pp.7–10 (p.8).

25 Ibid.

26 Ibid., p.9.

27 Ibid., p.10.

28 W.H. Auden and Louis MacNeice, 'Auden and MacNeice: Their Last Will and Testament', in W.H. Auden and Louis MacNeice *Letters from Iceland* (London: Faber, 1937), pp.236–58 (p.241).

29 Wilfred Owen, 'Preface' in Wilfred Owen, *Poems* (London: Chatto and Windus, 1920), p.ix. MacNeice first cites this in 'Subject in Modern Poetry', in *Essays and Studies* by Members of the English Association, collected by Helen Darbishire, 22 ([December] 1936), pp.144–58; repr. in *Literary Criticism*, pp.57–74 (p.63).

30 Louis MacNeice, *Modern Poetry: A Personal Essay* (London: Oxford University Press, 1938), p.79.

31 Louis MacNeice, 'Eclogue by a Five-Barred Gate (*Death and two Shepherds*)', pp.10–14 (p.11).

32 Ibid., p.12.

33 Louis MacNeice. 'Ode', pp.32–7 (p.34).

34 Ibid., p.36.

35 Ibid., p.37.

36 Louis MacNeice, 'Some Notes on Mr Yeats' Plays', *New Verse*, 18 (December 1935), pp.7–9 (p.9).

37 John Engle, 'A Modest Refusal: Yeats, MacNeice, and Irish Poetry', in Deborah Fleming (ed.), *Learning the Trade: Essays on W. B. Yeats and Contemporary Poetry* (West Cornwall: Locust Hill Press, 1993), pp.71–88 (p.73). For more on the Yeats–MacNeice relationship during this period and immediately afterwards, see, Richard Danson Brown, 'Neutrality and Commitment: MacNeice, Yeats, Ireland and the Second World War', *Journal of Modern Literature*, 28:3 (spring 2005), pp.109–29.

38 I.M. Parsons, 'Mr. MacNeice's Poems', rev. of *Poems* by Louis MacNeice (London: Faber, 1935), *The Spectator*, 5597 (4 October 1935), pp.518–19 (p.518).

39 Ibid., p.519. MacNeice might not have been impressed by Parson's review, and in their 'Last Will and Testament' MacNeice and Auden expressed the joint hope, 'May the critic I.M. Parsons feel at last / A creative impulse'. [Auden and MacNeice, 'Last Will and Testament', p.247.]

40 W.B. Yeats, 'Introduction', in *The Oxford Book of Modern Poetry* (Oxford: Oxford University Press, 1936), p.xxxvi.

41 Ibid., p.xxxviii. The MacNeice poems selected by Yeats were 'The Individualist Speaks', 'Turf-stacks', 'Circe' and 'An Eclogue for Christmas'. See, Robert Alden Rubin, 'Some Heroic Discipline: William Butler Yeats and the *Oxford Book of Modern Verse*', unpub. PhD diss., University of North Carolina at Chapel Hill, 2011, pp.323–41.

42 Louis MacNeice, 'Turf-stacks', pp.15–16 (p.16).

43 Louis MacNeice, 'Letter to Graham and Anne Shepard', in *Letters from Iceland*, pp.31–5 (p.32).

44 Louis MacNeice, 'Hetty to Nancy', in *Letters from Iceland*, pp.156–99 (pp.179–80). The Latin is from Juvenal's *Satire*, I, l.74. Usually translated as 'honesty is praised and starves', but on occasion rendered, as MacNeice seems here to intend, as 'honesty is praised and is left out in the cold'. Juvenal, *Satire* I, in Morton Braund, ed. and trans., *Juvenal and Persius* Loeb Classical Library 91 (Cambridge: Belknap, 2004), pp.130–45 (p.136).

45 MacNeice, 'Hetty to Nancy', p.157. [Italics in the original.]

46 W.J.P., 'B.U.D.S.' rev. of performance 'Station Bell' by Louis MacNeice, *The Mermaid* (March 1937), p.71.

47 Ibid.

48 Ibid.

49 J. Michael Walton, 'Translation or Transubstantiation?', in Fiona Macintosh, Pantelis Michelakis, Edith Hall and Oliver Taplin (eds), *Agamemnon in Performance 458 BC to AD 2004* (Oxford: Oxford University Press, 2005), pp.189–206 (p.196).

50 Qtd in ibid., p.196.

51 Ibid.

52 Ibid.

53 Walton describing the reconstruction of the production notes in Michael J. Sidnell, 'Another "Death of Tragedy": Louis MacNeice's Translation of *Agamemnon* in the Context of his Work in the Theatre', in Martin Cropp, Elaine Fantham, S. E. Scully (eds), *Greek Tragedy and its Legacy: Essays Presented to D. J. Conacher* (Calgary: University of Calgary Press, 1986), pp.323–35.

54 F.R. Earp., 'The *Agamemnon* and the *Bacchae* in English verse', rev. of *The Agamemnon of Aeschylus,* trans. Louis MacNeice (London: Faber, 1936) and of *The Bacchae of Euripides*, trans. Francis Evelyn (London: Heath Cranton, 1936), *The Classical Review*, 51:4 (Sept. 1937), pp.119–120 (p.119).

55 Louis MacNeice, *Out of the Picture* (Faber: London, 1937), p.9.

56 Ibid.

57 Louis MacNeice, *I Crossed the Minch* (London: Longmans, Green, 1938; repr. Edinburgh: Polygon, 2007), p.180.

58 Robert Louis Stephenson, *Strange Case of Dr Jekyll and Mr Hyde* (London: 1886).

59 MacNeice, *Out of the Picture*, p.76.

60 Ibid.

61 Ibid., p.77.

62 'Sumer Is Icumen In' is a medieval English rota of the mid-13th century.

63 MacNeice, *Out of the Picture*, pp.77–8.

64 Ibid., p.79.

65 MacNeice, *Minch*, pp.26–7.

66 Ibid., p.23.

67 Ibid., p.129. [Italics in the original.]

68 Louis MacNeice, 'The Play and the Audience' in *Footnotes to the Theatre*, ed. R. D. Charques (London: Peter Davies, 1938), pp.32–43; repr. in *Literary Criticism*, pp.87–97 (p.87). In one of those turns of irony of which it is quite possible to make too much, MacNeice's essay was preceded by one of the same title by St John Greer Ervine.

69 Ibid., p.92.

70 Louis MacNeice, *Zoo* (London: Michael Joseph, 1938; repr. London: Faber, 2013).

71 Louis MacNeice, 'Carrickfergus', pp.55–6 (p.56).

72 Louis MacNeice, 'June Thunder', p.57.

73 Ibid.

74 Louis MacNeice, 'The Sunlight on the Garden', pp.57–8 (p.57).

75 Louis MacNeice, 'Eclogue from Iceland', pp.72–82 (pp.81–2).

76 Louis MacNeice, 'Leaving Barra', pp.88–9 (p.89).

77 Louis MacNeice, 'Rugby Football Excursion', in *The Earth Compels* (London: Faber, 1938), pp.60–1 (p.60). MacNeice omitted this poem, uniquely of those in *The Earth Compels*, from all but the first of the selected poems he oversaw in his life.

78 Ibid., p.60.

79 Louis MacNeice, 'Postscript to Iceland *for W.H. Auden*', pp.96–98 (p.98).

80 MacNeice, *Minch*, p.178.

81 MacNeice, 'Eclogue from Iceland', p.78.

82 Ibid.

83 Auden and MacNeice, 'Auden and MacNeice: Their Last Will and Testament', in *Letters from Iceland*, p.236.

84 Clive James, 'Preface' to 'Poem of the Year', in *The Book of My Enemy: Collected Verse 1958–2003* (London: Picador, 2003) pp.247–9 (p.247).

CHAPTER 6

Autumn Journal

By the summer of 1938, MacNeice was sure of the truth of his earlier prediction that 'soon, my friend, | We shall have no time for dances'.[1] As time ran out, he continued to stress that 'poets are not legislators',[2] but their role, nonetheless, was increasingly important as 'they put facts and feelings in italics, which makes people think about them and such thinking may in the end have an outcome in action'.[3] MacNeice suspected that 'if we are not interested in changing [the world], there is really very little to describe'.[4] This was a sensibility one American critic had noted as a strength of *The Earth Compels*, the work of a poet who 'has not … been willing to make a rather hasty burnt-offering to any single group … He has attempted to make a significant order which will include the quotidian, and which will permit him to retain his own identity in this order'.[5] MacNeice had 'the ability to make the present of more than temporary significance'.[6]

The last quarter of 1938 found MacNeice trying to shape the quotidian of the present into a whole that would frame

> the dead leaves falling, the burning bonfire,
> The dying that brings forth
> The harder life, revealing the tree's girders,
> The frost that kills the germs of *laissez-faire*.[7]

Autumn 1938 would mark more than the coming of winter. It would be the end of the hope of peace. And even though on 30 September

1938 'Chamberlain signed on the line and we all relapsed',[8] the sense of foreboding grew worse, the anticipation getting increasingly hard to bear.

Autumn 1938 was also a time of endings for MacNeice. He was done with the sort of prose work 'for which I had no vocation but which, I thought, to myself, I could do as well as the next man'.[9] His affair with Nancy Sharp had apparently ended in as dizzying a manner as it had been conducted. In Ireland, his father's potential candidacy for the primacy of all Ireland had floundered on succession rules which would have left the 76-year-old dean of Armagh bishop of a diocese so large and demanding that Bishop MacNeice had argued for its disuniting.[10] When his son sat down to write the long poem that would be published as *Autumn Journal*, the MacNeice family on both sides of the Irish Sea seemed largely settled, with only Dan in transit, sometimes with his grandparents, sometimes with his aunt and uncle and sometimes with his father.

MacNeice had earlier noted that 'the best poems are written on two or more planes at once, just as they are written from a multitude of motives. Poetry is essentially ambiguous, but ambiguity is not necessarily obscure'.[11] *Autumn Journal* would be a test of that claim, and he 'trust[ed the poem] contains some "criticism of life" or implies some standards which are not merely personal'.[12] It was, he said, 'both a panorama and a confession of faith'.[13]

The poem opens with MacNeice returning to London from a visit to Wickham, Hampshire, to see his father and stepmother, who were visiting Bea's eldest sister, Helena, widow of Admiral Sir Robert Swinburne Lowry, who had held from 1913 until his death in 1920 the title of Commander-in-Chief, Rosyth, the senior operational naval position in Scotland. Dan had come to Hampshire with his grandparents and nurse, and Louis's visit was typical of the relationship father, son and grandparents were having at the time. It was not just Bishop MacNeice whose social world had expanded significantly with his marriage to Bea, and we can tend to forget that Louis, too, now had family ties intimately connected with the Anglo-Irish elite. MacNeice had once recommended going to the zoo 'in the same spirit of tolerant but entirely unenvious admiration in which we go to tea with our inflexibly Victorian great-aunts',[14] but such a tone could not hide the depth of the connections he relied upon in the years immediately after his wife's departure and until the end of the war.

He was accompanied on the trip by Betsy, a borzoi, whom in *Zoo* he identified as having eyes 'neither human nor doggy, but like [those] of a film star',[15] which might help delineate the character of Clara de Groot, the

actress at the heart of one of the plots of *Out of the Picture*. By the time of
Autumn Journal, the adjectives are sharper:

> My dog, a symbol of the abandoned order,
>   Lies on the carriage floor,
> Her eyes inept and glamorous as a film star's,
>   Who wants to live, i.e. wants more
> Presents, jewellery, furs, gadgets, solicitations.[16]

While the 'train's rhythm becomes the *ad nauseam* repetition | Of every
tired aubade and madrigal',[17] recalling the earlier trains that had traversed
his poetry, the train, like all trains, must be going somewhere and dark
though the future looked it was still the future and still in some important
degree undecided.

The world might have been rushing to war, but MacNeice had his
private nightmares still, 'afraid in the web of night', with the roar of
the lions from London Zoo penetrating the dark wherein 'the gods are
absent and the men are still'.[18] But the personal here is also the public, the
individual life representative of a shared experience:

> I must go out to-morrow as the others do
>   And build the falling castle;
> Which has never fallen, thanks
>
>   ....
>
>   to the human animal's endless courage.[19]

The news might not have been full of propitious omens, but the man
who could not bring himself to join causes refused to concede that hope
was lost completely. He looked not to his father's faith but to his father's
example, hoping that 'a better Kingdom come' that 'in time may find its
body in men's bodies, | Its law and order in their heart's accord'.[20] Where
William Temple and his father saw the necessity of faith, because 'apart
from faith in God there really is nothing to be said for the notion of human
equality',[21] MacNeice acknowledged that a secular desire for a more equal
society was difficult precisely because

>   It is so hard to imagine
>   A world where the many would have their chance without
> A fall in the standard of intellectual living
>   And nothing left that the highbrow cared about.[22]

Nonetheless, he resolved to 'suppress' such 'fears', for

> There is no reason for thinking
> That, if you give a chance to people to think or live,
> The arts of thought or life will suffer and become rougher
> And not return more than you could ever give.[23]

All of which is redolent of his father's call for economic and social justice:

> The assumption that a man's life may be a private affair, that a man's life consisteth in the abundance of the things that he possesseth, that an individual who has acquired wealth – in part through the toil of others – may be unconcerned as to the circumstances governing the lives of those others, the character of the houses in which they may have to live, their sense of insecurity in employment and their fear of coming days when strength to toil may be no longer theirs; and that he can use or not use, in any way he pleases, retain or dispose of his money, independently, just as he himself thinks best – this conception of life, I venture to say, is as clearly a denial of Christ as is Russian Communism or German Fascism.[24]

In the face of such injustices, the 'worst of all | Deceits is to murmur "Lord, I am not worthy" | And, lying easy, turn your face to the wall'.[25] Across the opening three cantos the most insistent claim of *Autumn Journal* is established, that it is the responsibility of one who has the privilege and so the opportunity to ensure 'my feet follow my wider glance | First no doubt to stumble, then to walk with the others | And in the end – with time and luck – to dance'.[26]

It was not just a looming war that made autumn a time of more than falling leaves. His memory of the high points of the relationship with Sharp informs two of the great love poems in English from the twentieth century, cantos IV and XI of *Autumn Journal*. Even here, MacNeice took from the personal the need to confront the fact it was no longer permissible to prevaricate:

> it is on the strength of knowing you
> I reckon generous feeling more important
> Than the mere deliberating what to do

When neither the pros nor cons affect the pulses.[27]

Being alive meant being engaged with both the public and the private, for the private was no longer exempt from broader moral questions:

> posters flapping on the railings tell the fluttered
> World that Hitler speaks, that Hitler speaks
> And we cannot take it in and we go to our daily
> Jobs to the dull refrain of the caption 'War'.[28]

Whatever one may wish,

> it is no good saying
> 'Take away this cup';[29]
> Having helped to fill it ourselves it is only logic
> That now we should drink it up.
> Nor can we hide our heads in the sands, the sands have
> Filtered away.[30]

This was the conundrum Bishop Sterling Berry had addressed in 1915 and that MacNeice's father had identified as the failing of all the Irish churches when he argued that

> It is probably true that the majorities in the countries that became belligerent [in World War I], did not desire war. The majorities were not organised: The Churches had not put sufficient emphasis on their message. The militant forces which represented minorities were organised … It was too late to work for peace when war had begun.[31]

His son rejected the idea the solution might have been found in the churches, but he was as aware as his father that failure to prevent what in retrospect seemed inevitable was a failure of will enabled by those who had not applied their talents where they might best have served a purpose:

> The poet … should be synoptic and elastic in his sympathies. It is quite possible therefore that at some period his duty as a poet may conflict with his duties as a man. In that case he can stop writing, but he must not degrade his poetry even in the service of a good cause.[32]

It may risk bathos to associate the writing of poetry with the profession of faith, but the sentiment is essentially the same: There is a higher calling that can advance the cause of the whole and assert the integrity of the individual. Whatever the times might seem to demand, 'we might remember,' MacNeice had noted in 1937, 'that man is a ζῷον [living being] as well as πολιτιχὸν [a political being] and that quite a number of people have an organic sympathy with trees, mountains, flowers, or with a painting by Chardin', but that does not necessarily 'lessen our sympathy with our fellow human beings'.[33] But the risk in putting the 'painting by Chardin' ahead of the human is that one will forget 'a still life is alive | And in your Chardin the appalling unrest of the soul | Exudes from the dried fish and the brown jug and the bowl'.[34] MacNeice had been to Spain with Anthony Blunt – their last significant expedition together – in the months before the civil war broke out, walking 'around the ramparts', visiting museums, 'glibly talk[ing] | Of how the Spaniards lack all sense of business', and 'we thought the papers a lark | With their party politics and blank invective'.[35] Such sentiments then could serve as a reminder in 1938 of the cost of putting Chardin ahead of the 'unrest of the soul'.

In London in 1938 there was 'no time to doubt | If the puzzle really has an answer',[36] and at home on Primrose Hill the private man confronted the fact there would be 'No more looking at the view from the seats beneath the branches, | ... | They want the crest of this hill for anti-aircraft'.[37] He was unsure whether

> From now on I need take
> The trouble to go out choosing stuff for curtains
>   As I don't know anyone to make
> Curtains quickly.[38]

This might be the stuff of the quotidian and the mundane, but it was no longer trivial. MacNeice's marriage had begun in innocence when a commitment to aesthetics and Pure Form still seemed possible and had ended as such hopes were proving untenable:

> There were lots of things undone
>   But nobody cared, for the days were early.
> Nobody niggled, nobody cared,
>   ....

> We drove round Shropshire in a bijou car –
>> Bewdley, Cleobury, Mortimer, Ludlow –
> And the map of England was a toy bazaar
>> And the telephone wires were idle music.[39]

Now, the maps were matters of defensive redoubts and mustering spots for a soon to be re-invigorated Territorial Army.[40] Then,

>> roads ran easy, roads ran gay
>> Clear of the city and we together
> Could put on tweeds for a getaway
>> South or west to Clee or the Cotswolds;[41]

But 'That was then and now is now',[42] and back in Birmingham on 'a passing visit' he found 'No wife, no ivory tower, no funk-hole'.[43] At the hippodrome he saw George Formby and Florrie Forde reassuring everyone that all was well, though no one thought it was. The double-act took place on 28 September and the next day Adolf Hitler, Neville Chamberlain, Benito Mussolini and Édouard Daladier agreed to sign the Munich Agreement:

> The crisis is put off and things look better
> And we feel negotiation is not in vain –
>> Save my skin and damn my conscience.[44]

In October, MacNeice would return to lecturing the women of Bedford College on the ancient Greeks, and the first half of canto IX offers a technically exuberant and playful summation of the classics syllabus in its entirety. 'Conscious – long before Engels – of necessity | And therein free' the ancient Greeks 'plotted out their life with truism and humour',[45] but what lesson was to be learned from this when 'these dead are dead'? And

>> how one can imagine oneself among them
> I do not know;
> It was all so unimaginably different
>> And all so long ago.[46]

Thoughts of the new term inevitably brought back memories of his own schooling, of the truth that 'the great thing about public school is that life comes as quite a nice surprise'.[47] The other great surprise of the English public school system is that in some sort of Marxist irony it contains the seeds if not of its own destruction at least of its own disturbance, for

> sometimes a whisper in books
> Would challenge the code, or a censored memory sometimes,
> Sometimes the explosion of rooks,
> Sometimes the mere batter of light on the senses.
> And the critic jailed in the mind would peep through the grate
> And husky from long silence, murmur gently
> That there is something rotten in the state
> Of Denmark but the state is not the whole of Denmark.[48]

Although the 'critic did not win, has not won yet',[49] he might gain strength from the 'many better men outside | Than ever answered roll-call' at school.[50]

For the moment, Sharp still offered the most immediate model for the type of person who could live outside the 'system', whatever that system might be. Despite her own education at Cheltenham Ladies' College, that most elite of girls' schools, she was one for whom Auden had wished 'a call | To go on a dangerous mission for a fellow creature',[51] was one of those whose

> instinct
> Sanctions all you do,
> Who know that truth is nothing in abstraction,
> That action makes both wish and principle come true.[52]

There was no purpose denying individuality to defeat an enemy that denied individuality, and in people such as Sharp MacNeice saw the possibility of a way beyond his natural scepticism:

> All that I would like to be is human, having a share
> In a civilised, articulate and well-adjusted
> Community where the mind is given its due
> But the body is not distrusted.[53]

Perhaps he was not that far after all, from Virginia Woolf's position that a contemporary poet should

> never think yourself singular, never think your own case much harder than other people's. I admit that the age we live in makes this difficult … Think of yourself rather as something much humbler and less spectacular, but to my mind, far more interesting – a poet in whom live all the poets of the past, from whom all poets in time to come will spring … In short you are an immensely ancient, complex, and continuous character.[54]

In that same essay, Woolf had suggested that

> if you want to satisfy all those senses that rise in a swarm whenever we drop a poem among them – the reason, the imagination, the eyes, the ears, the palms of the hands and the soles of the feet, not to mention a million more that the psychologists have yet to name, you will do well to embark upon a long poem in which people as unlike yourself as possible talk at the tops of their voices. And for heaven's sake, publish nothing before you are thirty.[55]

MacNeice turned 31 while writing *Autumn Journal*. He had published a substantial amount before he was 30, and in a May 1940 lecture to the Workers' Educational Association Woolf deployed brilliantly selective quotation from *Autumn Journal* to mock a work she described as 'feeble as poetry', marred by 'the influence of films' and by 'the influence of poets such as Mr Yeats and Mr Eliot [which] explains the lack of transitions … and the violently opposed contrasts.'[56] Responding to her critique, MacNeice would bristle at her dismissal of the 'self-pity' she found in his work and that of his contemporaries:

> Self-pity? Of course our work embodied some self-pity. But look at Mrs Woolf's beloved nineteenth century. 'Anger, pity, scapegoat beating, excuse finding' – she intones against the poor lost Thirties; you find all those things – in full measure and running over – in the Romantic Revival … My generation at least put some salt in it. And we never, even at our most martyred, produced such a holocaust of self-pity as Shelley in *Adonais*.[57]

The self-mocking classicist headed back to Oxford to do something he had not done before: get involved in electoral politics, driving voters to the polls in the pivotal Oxford by-election. Quintin Hogg, the son of Lord Hailsham, then the Lord Chancellor, and about as quintessential a representative of Conservative orthodoxy as one could get, was standing against Sandy Lindsay, the Master of Balliol, on whose behalf both the Labour and Liberal candidates had stood down. The campaign was essentially a referendum on the Munich Agreement. MacNeice was easing himself into active participation in causes, moving beyond the 'mere deliberating what to do',[58] aware at last

> that those who by their habit hate
> Politics can no longer keep their private
> Values unless they open the public gate
> To a better political system.[59]

In a tough lesson, 'Thursday came and Oxford went to the polls | And made its coward vote', but he was resolved that 'From now on | Each occasion must be used, however trivial, | To rally the ranks of those whose chance will soon be gone.'[60]

Whatever MacNeice's professed resolve, the reality was that he retreated to London, to 'Shelley and jazz and lieder and love and hymn-tunes'.[61] He thought to 'get drunk among the roses',[62] but there was not sufficient bulwark against the encroaching nightmare. The jazz and the lieder and all the other diversions could not divert attention from ghosts who bore witness to what had come and what would come. They could not deny the continuing stark horror of Charles Sorley's sonnet:

> When you see millions of the mouthless dead
> Across your dreams in pale battalions go,
> Say not soft things as other men have said,
> That you'll remember. For you need not so.
> Give them not praise. For, deaf, how should they know
> It is not curses heaped on each gashed head?
> Nor tears. Their blind eyes see not your tears flow.
> Nor honour. It is easy to be dead.
> Say only this, 'They are dead.' Then add thereto,

'Yet many a better one has died before.'
Then, scanning all the overcrowded mass, should you
Perceive one face that you loved heretofore,
It is a spook. None wears the face you knew.
Great death has made all this for evermore.[63]

MacNeice reported that the ghosts had returned:

        I cannot see their faces
    Walking in file, slowly in file;
They have no shoes on their feet, the knobs of their ankles
      Catch the moonlight as they pass the stile
And cross the moor among the skeletons of bog-oak
      Following the track from the gallows back to town;
Each has the end of a rope around his neck. I wonder
    Who let these men come back, who cut them down –.[64]

Although he hoped 'They are sure to go away if we take no notice',[65] he knew that after frantic storytelling, music playing and philosophising nothing was likely to have changed:

      You may look, I think the coast is clear.
  Well, why don't you answer?
    I can't answer because they are still there.[66]

Nightmares and ghosts of recent wars invoked further reflection on the Ireland he had tried so hard to dismiss in 'Valediction' but about which he now had more nuanced feelings. 'I thought I was well | Out of it, educated and domiciled in England', but 'her name keeps ringing like a bell'.[67] Perhaps presciently in light of his attempts to secure the chair of English at Trinity College, Dublin, the following year and his taking up of an Irish passport upon the outbreak of war, MacNeice suggested that Ireland's charms were not just those of Yeats's mythical country, 'members of a world that never was, | Baptised with fairy water', but that Ireland was a place where 'one feels that here at least one can | Do local work which is not at the world's mercy',[68] however mistaken its 'assumption that everyone cares | Who is the king of your castle.'[69] Nonetheless, he identified in a perfectly drawn couplet the challenge Éire would confront once war was declared, 'A cart that is drawn by somebody else's horse | And carrying goods to somebody else's market.'[70]

As the year waned, it became harder and harder to pretend the Munich Agreement had reversed the inevitable, but domestic concerns still mattered, and if earlier MacNeice had echoed Sorley, now he looked to William Blake's 'Jerusalem' with its opening questions:

> And did those feet in ancient time
> Walk upon Englands mountains green:
> And was the holy Lamb of God,
> On Englands pleasant pastures seen!
>
> And did the Countenance Divine,
> Shine forth upon our clouded hills?
> And was Jerusalem builded here,
> Among these dark Satanic Mills?[71]

MacNeice was surer of the answer to the question posed in the first verse than was Blake, asserting confidently that 'In the days that were early the music came easy | On cradle and coffin, in the corn and the barn.'[72] But, like Blake, MacNeice saw a 'country [now] a dwindling annexe to the factory, | Squalid as an after-birth', a country 'tight and narrow, teeming with unwanted | Children who are so many'.[73] The cost of past wars and industrialisation was visible all around:

> Beneath the standard lights; the paralytic winding
>   His barrel-organ sprays the passers-by
> With April music; the many-ribboned hero
>   With half a lung or a leg waits his turn to die.[74]

1938 was a year that would 'leave a heavy | Overdraft to its heir', its legacy 'The devil quoting scripture, the traitor, the coward, the thug | Eating dinner in the name of peace and progress'.[75] It would leave behind the stark reality of

> hordes of homeless poor running the gauntlet
>   In hostile city streets of white and violet lamps
> Whose flight is without a terminus but better
>   Than the repose of concentration camps.[76]

And worst of all, it would leave the echoes of the calls for help which had been ignored, 'Come over, they said, into Macedonia and help us' but 'the chance is gone'.[77]

Other things had changed, too, and MacNeice at last admitted 'the lady is gone who stood in the way so long',[78] and so Sharp went from being a major part of his life to one of the bundle of memories that make a life, infatuation defeated by her refusal to continue an affair with no positive outcome in sight. Alone and weary, MacNeice was in London as December opened while Auden was in Brussels with Christopher Isherwood, where he wrote 'Musée des Beaux Arts' with its compelling opening, 'About suffering they were never wrong, | The Old Masters'.[79] Coincidentally, MacNeice walked past the closed National Gallery in Trafalgar Square and reflected on the lessons contained in the paintings there, suggesting that the Old Masters were wrong about quite a lot: 'Sebastian calmly waiting the next arrow' and all the other 'paradigm[s] | Of life's successions, treacheries, recessions; | The unfounded confidence of the dead'.[80] It was 'A week to Christmas', a time for which his sister said Louis 'never lost [his] reverence … and to the end of his life he tried year after year to recreate the spirit of those early Rectory Christmases, often, I am afraid, sad because he never quite could'.[81] No wonder that at times he could sound a bleaker moral note than his father:

> And Conscience still goes crying through the desert
> 　　With sackcloth round his loins:
> A week to Christmas – hark the herald angels
> 　　Beg for copper coins.[82]

Nonetheless, MacNeice sought comfort in the affirmation that 'the total cause outruns the mere condition',[83] and he wondered

> 　　　　　What is the use
> Of the minor loyalty – 'Dear city of Cecrops',
> Unless we have also the wider franchise, can answer
> 　　'Dear city of Zeus'?[84]

But even this was not so much a testament to faith as an exposition of acceptance, relying on Marcus Aurelius's assertion that

Everything harmonizes with me, which is harmonious to thee, O Universe. Nothing for me is too early nor too late, which is in due time for thee. Everything is fruit to me which thy seasons bring, O Nature: from thee are all things, in thee are all things, to thee all things return. The poet says, Dear City of Cecrops; and wilt not thou say, Dear City of Zeus?[85]

Along with Aurelius, Francis of Assisi was also summoned, identified as 'the grey saint'. Looking to find reassurance amidst the distress, MacNeice quoted St Francis: 'Praised be thou, O Lord, for our brother the sun', evoking the saint's 'Canticle of the Sun'. Composed when he was believed to be near death, the canticle is as close to stoic pantheism as any Christian would come and so staked out a position more appealing to MacNeice than would have a traditional Christian invocation.[86]

Addressing Sharp one last time, MacNeice acknowledged that 'I know you find these phrases high falutin',[87] but reassured by her vitality he admitted that

> while I sympathise
> With the wish to quit, to make the great refusal,
> I feel that such a defeat is also treason,
> That deaths like these are lies.
> A fire should be left burning
> Till it burns itself out:
> We shan't have another chance to dance and shout
> Once the flames are silent.[88]

As the year edged ever closer to an end, MacNeice went south again to Spain, this time to offer testament on behalf of a besieged Barcelona. En route, in France, he was reminded of the attractions that had once seduced him as an undergraduate, the idea that a 'sensible man must keep his aesthetic | And his moral standards apart'.[89] That would not do in December 1938, and in Spain he came 'to a place in space where shortly | All of us may be forced to camp in time'.[90] Yet in Barcelona, MacNeice found the validation of his humanist inclinations, identifying, whether accurately or not, a place where 'the soul has found its voice | Though not indeed by choice'.[91] The end of the year and the evidence of Barcelona brought a more pressing message:

> I must make amends
> And try to correlate event with instinct
>   And me with you or you and you with all,
>   ....
> I have loved defeat and sloth,
>   The tawdry halo of the idle martyr;
> I have thrown away the roots of will and conscience,
>   Now I must look for both.[92]

Again, he picked up on the practical component of his father's faith, who had told his diocese in a June 1936 pastoral letter that

> I am not asking any man to abandon the party or group to which by conviction he is attached, but I am asking every man, who is avowedly Christian, to make sure that his loyalty to his party does not conflict with his loyalty to his Lord. Not one of us has the right to dictate to another what his party allegiance should be, but anyone would have the right to reproach us if, while we professed to be followers of Christ, we disregarded His example.[93]

He was getting ever closer to admitting publicly the potential of his father's faith, if still determinedly opposed to the validity of its foundation story:

> And you, who work for Christ, and you, as eager
>   For a better life, humanist, atheist,
> And you, devoted to a cause, and you, to a family,
>   Sleep and may your beliefs and zeal persist.[94]

With war coming, MacNeice now looked to the justification for joining the fight. With his father, he asserted that that justification could not simply be to oppose what we do not want. It had to be affirmative of a cause worth embracing, aimed at creating

>   a possible land
>   Not of sleep-walkers, not of angry puppets,
> But where both heart and brain can understand
>   The movements of our fellows;
> Where life is a choice of instruments and none

Is debarred his natural music.

....

Where the people are more than a crowd.[95]

Autumn Journal was summative of a life and career coming to an end. It was anticipatory, albeit with nervous uncertainty, of a life and career to come. It was an assertion of a determined hope sympathetic to that expressed by Spike Milligan in early 1944, who, thinking he would die in the Italian campaign, proposed for himself the epitaph: 'I died for the England I dreamed of, not the England I knew.'[96]

NOTES

References to the poems of Louis MacNeice are as they appear in Peter McDonald (ed.), *Collected Poems* (London: Faber, 2007), except as noted.

1   Louis MacNeice, 'The Sunlight on the Garden', pp.57–8 (p.57).
2   Louis MacNeice to W.H. Auden, 21 October 1937, p.304. The letter was published in *New Verse*, 26 and 27 (November 1937), pp.11–12.
3   Ibid.
4   Ibid., p.305.
5   Samuel French Morse, rev. of *The Earth Compels* by Louis MacNeice (London: Faber, 1938), *Poetry*, 53:5 (February 1939), pp.280–3 (p.280).
6   Ibid., p.282.
7   Louis MacNeice, *Autumn Journal*, I, p.102.
8   Louis MacNeice, *The Strings Are False: An Unfinished Autobiography*, ed. E.R. Dodds (London: Faber, 1966), p.175.
9   Ibid., p.173.
10 The diocese would finally be separated into two on 1 January 1945, three years after MacNeice's death, when Charles King Irwin relinquished Down and Dromore while continuing as Bishop of Connor. William Kerr became Bishop of Down and Dromore.
11 Louis MacNeice, 'Poetry To-day', in Geoffrey Grigson (ed.), *The Arts To-day* (London: John Lane, 1935), pp.25–67; repr. in Alan Heuser (ed.), *Selected Literary Criticism of Louis MacNeice* (Oxford: Clarendon, 1987), pp.10–43 (p.43).
12 Louis MacNeice, 'Note' to *Autumn Journal*, in *Collected Poems*, ed. Peter McDonald (London: Faber, 2007), p.791.
13 Louis MacNeice to T.S. Eliot, [29?] November 1938, p.312.
14 Louis MacNeice, *Zoo* (London: Michael Joseph, 1938; repr. London: Faber, 2013), p.32.
15 Ibid., p.75.
16 MacNeice, *Autumn Journal*, I, p.102.
17 Ibid.
18 Ibid., II, p.103.

19 Ibid., p.104.
20 Ibid., III, p.105.
21 William Temple, *Christianity and the Social Order* (Harmondsworth: Penguin, 1941), p.15.
22 MacNeice, *Autumn Journal*, III, p.106.
23 Ibid.
24 John Frederick MacNeice, '"Russian Communism, German Fascism", Inaugural Service of the Diocesan Council of Youth. Sermon Preached in St Anne's Cathedral, Belfast, on Wednesday, May 3rd, 1933', in John Frederick MacNeice, *Some Northern Churchmen, and Some Notes on the Church in Belfast* (Belfast: Erskine Mayne; Dublin: Church of Ireland, 1934) pp.48–59 (p.57).
25 MacNeice, *Autumn Journal*, III, p.106. The reference is to Matt. 8:8 ['The centurion answered and said, Lord, I am not worthy that thou shouldest come under my roof: but speak the word only, and my servant shall be healed'].
26 Ibid. pp.106–7.
27 Ibid., IV, pp.108–9.
28 Ibid., V, p.109.
29 The reference is to Mark 14:36 ['And he said, Abba, Father, all things are possible unto thee; take away this cup from me: nevertheless not what I will, but what thou wilt'].
30 MacNeice, *Autumn Journal*, V, p.111.
31 John Frederick MacNeice, *Carrickfergus and Its Contacts: Some Chapters in the History of Ulster* (London: Simpkin, Marshall; Belfast: Erskine Mayne, 1928), p.83.
32 Louis MacNeice, 'A Statement', *New Verse*, 31–32 (autumn 1938), p.7; repr. in *Literary Criticism*, p.98.
33 Louis MacNeice, rev. of *The Note-Books and Papers of Gerard Manley Hopkins*, ed. Humphrey House (London: Oxford University Press, 1937); repr. in *Literary Criticism*, pp.79–83 (pp.81–2).
34 Louis MacNeice, 'Nature Morte (*Even so it is not easy to be dead*)', p.23.
35 MacNeice, *Autumn Journal*, VI, p.113.
36 Ibid., VII, p.115.
37 Ibid.
38 Ibid., p.116.
39 Ibid., VIII, p.117.
40 'Doubling the Territorial Army.' Second Leader. *The Times*, 30 March 1939, p.15.
41 MacNeice, *Autumn Journal*, VIII, p.118.
42 Ibid.
43 Ibid., pp.118–19.
44 Ibid., p.119.
45 Ibid., IX, p.120.
46 Ibid., p.122.
47 Nancy Banks-Smith, 'The Dismal Diary of Adrienne Mole', *The Guardian*, 4 February 1994, in Alan Rusbridger (ed.), *The Guardian Year '94* (London: Fourth Estate, 1994), pp.237–40 (p.240).
48 MacNeice, *Autumn Journal*, X, p.124.

49   Ibid., p.125.

50   Ibid.

51   'Auden and MacNeice: Their Last Will and Testament', in W.H. Auden and Louis MacNeice, *Letters from Iceland* (London: Faber, 1937), pp.236–58 (p.253).

52   MacNeice, *Autumn Journal* XI, p.126.

53   Ibid., XII, p.129.

54   Virginia Woolf, 'A Letter to a Young Poet', in *The Death of the Moth, and Other Essays* (London: Hogarth, 1942), <http://ebooks.adelaide.edu.au/w/woolf/virginia/w91d/chapter25.html>, accessed 27 August 2014.

55   Ibid.

56   Virginia Woolf, 'The Leaning Tower', in *Folios of New Writing*, 2 (autumn 1940), pp.11–33 (p.23, p.26); repr. in *Collected Essays* Vol. 2 (London: Hogarth, 1967), pp.162–181 (p.172, p.175).

57   Louis MacNeice, 'The Tower that Once', in *Folios of New Writing*, 3 (spring 1941), pp.11–33; repr. in *Literary Criticism*, pp.119–24 (p.123).

58   Ibid., IV, pp.108–9.

59   Ibid., XIV, p.134.

60   Ibid.

61   Ibid., XV, p.135.

62   Ibid.

63   'A Sonnet', in Charles Sorley, *Marlborough and Other Poems* (Cambridge: Cambridge University Press, 1916), p.78. The poem is now commonly known as 'The Army of Death'. Like MacNeice, Sorley had been educated at Marlborough College (1908–13).

64   MacNeice, *Autumn Journal*, XV, p.136.

65   Ibid.

66   Ibid., p.137.

67   MacNeice, *Autumn Journal*, XVI, p.139.

68   Ibid.

69   Ibid., p.140.

70   Ibid., p.139.

71   William Blake, 'Preface' ['Jerusalem'] to *Milton: A Poem.* (London: 1804), <http://www.blakearchive.org/exist/blake/archive/comparison.xq?selection=compare&copies=all&bentleynum=B2&copyid=milton.a&java=> accessed 28 August 2014.

72   MacNeice, *Autumn Journal*, XVIII, p.144.

73   Ibid.

74   Ibid., p.145.

75   Ibid., p.146.

76   Ibid.

77   Ibid., p.146. 'Come over to Macedonia and help us' is a quote from Acts 16:9.

78   Ibid., XIX, p.148.

79   W.H. Auden, 'Palais des Beaux Arts', *New Writing*, ns II(*spring 1939*), p.2; repr. as 'Musée des Beaux Arts' in W.H. Auden, *Another Time: Poems* (New York: Random House, 1940), p.36.

80   MacNeice, *Autumn Journal*, XX, p.150.

81   Elizabeth Nicholson, 'Trees Were Green', in Terence Brown and Alec Reid (eds), *Time Was Away: The World of Louis MacNeice* (Dublin: Dolmen, 1974), pp.11–20 (p.12).

82   MacNeice, *Autumn Journal*, XX, p.152.

83   Ibid., p.153.

84   Ibid. According to Eusebius, Cecrops was the mythical king of Athens who deified Zeus and ordained sacrifices to be offered to him rather than the gods.

85   Marcus Aurelius, *The Thoughts of the Emperor Marcus Aurelius Antoninus*, trans. George Long (Boston: 1894), IV:23.

86   MacNeice, *Autumn Journal*, XXI, p.153. MacNeice paraphrases this second line and omits the overtly Christian opening line and the Christian aspects of this line as well: 'O most high, almighty, good Lord God, to thee belong praise, glory, honour, and all blessing! | Praised be my Lord God with all his creatures, and specially our brother the sun, who brings us the day and who brings us the light; fair is he and shines with a very great splendour: O Lord, he signifies to us thee!' St Francis of Assisi, *Laudes creaturarum* ['Canticle of the Sun'], <http://drc.usask.ca/projects/faulkner/main/related_texts/st_francis_canticle.html#1>, accessed 28 August 2014.

87   MacNeice, *Autumn Journal*, XXI, p.153.

88   Ibid., pp.154–5.

89   Ibid., XXII, p.157.

90   Ibid., XXIII, p.158.

91   Ibid., p.159.

92   Ibid., p.160.

93   John Frederick MacNeice, 'Pastoral Letter to the Members of the Church of Ireland in Belfast', in John Frederick MacNeice, *Our First Loyalty* (Belfast: Erskine Mayne, 1937), pp.83–6 (p.85–6).

94   MacNeice, *Autumn Journal*, XXIV, p.162.

95   Ibid., p.163.

96   Spike Milligan, *Mussolini: His Part in My Downfall*, ed. Jack Hobbs. (London: Michael Joseph, 1978), p.264. After the war, the British government denied Milligan citizenship on account of his having been born in India and a lack of evidence as to his Irish-born parents' British citizenship after Ireland's independence. Offered citizenship as an immigrant, Milligan refused on the grounds that six years in the British army during the war should have sufficed. He remained an Irish national until his death.

CHAPTER 7

The War Years

Then the war came. And war found MacNeice in Éire, where it was immediately announced that Irish policy would be one of strict neutrality. Éire had pinned its hopes on the League of Nations, and its leadership wondered now why Britain and France had taken a stand over Poland when other countries had not earlier been of such concern; these included Czechoslovakia, which following the Munich Agreement had been obliged, as if the bulk of the agreement were not bad enough, to surrender the city of Český Těšín to Poland, whose forces entered it on 2 October 1938. Anglo-French talk of treaty obligations rang hollow in Dublin.

Before the war, MacNeice had promised the Cuala Press a volume of poetry, so in the midst of larger personal and geopolitical upheaval he was focused on shaping his first Irish publication. The dedicatory poem offered a volume which was 'Nothing but odds and ends a thief | Bundled up in the last ditch,'[1] but the timing also meant the collection included his meditation on 'The Coming of War'. In Dublin in August 1939, MacNeice had reason yet again to re-evaluate his relationship with the country and the capital, which

> was never my town
> I was not born nor bred
> Nor schooled here and she will not
> Have me alive or dead
> But yet she holds my mind.[2]

He yearned for the 'glamour of her squalor, | The bravado of her talk',[3] but wondered

> if in a year
> Democracy will be dead
> Or what is more to the point –
> If I shall be dead.[4]

From Dublin, he and a friend, Ernst Stahl, made their way to Cushendun, County Antrim, where the MacNeice family had rented a house. As the news worsened, MacNeice and Stahl borrowed Elizabeth's car and headed for the family's mythic homeland, 'Hoping to hide my head | In the clouds of the West',[5] but when war was declared Stahl demanded they head to Dublin immediately so he could take the first boat to England. MacNeice drove him back but stayed on in Éire, 'drinking in a bar with Irish literary friends who, far from sharing his sense of catastrophe, only wanted to discuss variant versions of Irish street songs'.[6] On 3 September he went to Croke Park and watched the All-Ireland hurling final, 'Cork in crimson against Kerry in orange and black. Talk of escapism, I thought'.[7] He got the colours right but confused Kerry with Kilkenny, showing 'how little he felt at home, and how little he understood his surroundings'.[8]

Armed now with an Irish as well as a British passport and exempt from mandatory war work as a result of his birthplace, MacNeice stayed away from England, mainly in Belfast and its environs, where 'my family still had family prayers in the morning but the god of the house was the radio. "And that is the end of the news." But it never was'.[9] At times, he travelled south to Dublin to pursue, in rather desultory fashion, his options in Éire.

Irish neutrality might have been grounded in both moral and practical arguments, but, as Elizabeth Bowen noted, the declaration of neutrality was 'Éire's first free self-assertion'.[10] As such, 'far from being solely an act of isolationism, the declaration of neutrality led to a fundamental rethinking of Ireland's relationship to European culture and politics and to a new sense of national identity'.[11] Irish writers had a variety of responses both to neutrality and to those such as MacNeice who seemed to some to be claiming a degree of Irishness not hitherto visible. Those sentiments inspired one of the more famous, if now shrouded in confusion, cultural spats of early in the war. MacNeice either was or recently had been in Dublin, pursuing the possibility of appointment as professor of English at Trinity College, Dublin, when a 'wild hooey ... over Louis's erupted', as Patrick Kavanagh recounted in 'The Battle of the Palace Bar'.[12] Only fragments of 'The Battle' have survived, if, indeed, it was ever finished. Austin Clarke's dismissal of MacNeice's aspirations, 'Let him go back [to London] and labour for Faber and Faber', was countered by the perhaps unlikely person of Fred Higgins.[13] The dispute escalated, and 'They fought like barbarians, these highbrow grammarians | ... | And in no other land could a battle so grand | Have been fought over poetry, but in Ireland my dear!'[14] MacNeice himself cannot have helped matters given his ready acknowledgement that should he get the chair at Trinity – he did not – it 'would ... be an academic scandal'.[15]

Kavanagh came from the Ulster of which MacNeice was essentially ignorant: Catholic, agrarian and south of the border. On 12 October 1939 he appeared with Higgins and MacNeice on a Radio Éireann discussion, 'A Literary Night Out'.[16] The observation of the show's producer, Roibeárd Ó Faracháin, that 'poor Fred Higgins and poor Louis MacNeice, both good poets, both men of mind, could not at that time even half-master the very special business of largely impromptu live broadcasting' might well explain MacNeice's loyalty to scripted programming throughout his time at the BBC.[17] MacNeice did not forget Kavanagh, either, producing a 1960 reading of his seminal poem 'The Great Hunger' for BBC radio. Kavanagh provided the introduction.[18]

Higgins and MacNeice sparred over the appropriate nature of poetry throughout the 1930s, perhaps most scathingly in a 1932 radio broadcast when Higgins had asked, 'Do the poets of your school never sing?' to which MacNeice had responded, 'Do the poets of your school never think?'[19] By the time war approached, Higgins was making an appeal, elements of which were theoretically sympathetic to MacNeice's position:

> Present-day Irish poets are believers – heretical believers, maybe – but they have the spiritual buoyancy of a belief in something. The sort of belief I see in Ireland is a belief emanating from life, from nature, from revealed religion, and from the nation. A sort of dream that produces a sense of magic.[20]

But Higgins had included in this appeal to MacNeice the observation that 'as an Irishman [you] cannot escape from your blood, nor from your blood-music that brings the racial character to mind'.[21] MacNeice seized on this, asking if 'racial rhythm' was a better well-spring than 'extra-national rhythms' and suggesting that, if so, 'there is more likelihood of good poetry appearing among the Storm Troopers of Germany than in the cosmopolitan communities of Paris or New York'.[22] Yet a 'dream that produces a sense of magic' and 'heretical believers ... [who] have the spiritual buoyancy of a belief in something' are both fundamental elements of MacNeice's poetry. MacNeice would later memorialise Higgins in *Autumn Sequel* under the pseudonym Reilly:

> I knew one other poet who made his choice
> To sing and die, a meticulous maker too,
> To know whom too made all his friends rejoice
>
> In a hailfellow idyll, a ragout
> Of lyricism, and gossip; Reilly came
> From Connaught, and brown bogwater and blue
>
> Hills followed him through Dublin with the same
> Aura of knowing innocence, of earth
> That is alchemized by light.[23]

Whatever their wishes, Irish writers could not avoid questions of the cultural and social implications of Éire's neutrality. Denis Johnston, who would ultimately decide to become a BBC war correspondent, recalled in a manuscript memoir that in November 1943, with Allied forces in Italy,

> I had just been given a lecture ... on the evils of Irish neutrality – the text being that people who benefit from the blessings of justice and democracy ought to help in their preservation. Fair enough, if we really know that this is what we are fighting for. But do we know it? ... What that priest on the Sangro [River] said was true. Evil is like a Vampire. When you take arms against it and destroy it, you find in the end that you are evil too – that it is living on your own actions.[24]

The alternative, isolated neutrality, was not necessarily healthier, as Kate O'Brien recognised in her novel *The Last of Summer*, published in 1943 and looking back to the summer of 1939: 'Oh yes,' Jo Kernahan had explained to her visiting French cousin that summer, 'Éire will be neutral, which is only the clearest sense politically. But that's beside the point. Little patches of immunity like ours are going to be small consolation for what's coming.'[25]

In September 1939, MacNeice's own attitude was close to that which Éire's political leadership espoused: 'No need to apologise for our neutrality', Joseph Walsh, Secretary of the Department of External Affairs, told John J. Hearne, the High Commissioner in Canada: 'The countries at war are fighting for their own immediate material interests. Spiritual evils cannot be cured by the supreme evil of war.'[26] This echoed the language of MacNeice's father and mirrored some of MacNeice's own concerns. Indeed, Hearne would report that among those Irish voices he found most useful in aiding his case was that of the Catholic Bishop of Galway, Michael Browne, who had preached a sermon in County Galway warning those who might be tempted to use the war for their own ends that

> to invade a peaceful country like Ireland was not lawful war, but murder, and those who assisted in any way were guilty of the crime of murder before God. Not even the pretext of solving partition or securing unity would justify the crime of any Irishman in assisting any foreign power to invade his own land.[27]

The two bishops, Browne and MacNeice, would have been able to see eye to eye on almost no other point, but on this subject they spoke separately as if with one voice.

For MacNeice, as for his friend and mentor E.R. Dodds and as for his father, that Britain was entering a war quite evidently caused by a lack of principle over the previous twenty-five years made the existence of a neutral Irish state something of both a comfort and a rebuke. MacNeice shared the view of his cousin-by-marriage, Bowen, that 'Éire (and I think rightly) sees her neutrality as positive not merely negative.'[28] Additionally, for families such as the Bowens, Greers and MacNeices, Irish neutrality represented a sharp change from the First World War, especially from post-Easter 1916. Among those who recognised the differences was the British representative in Éire, Sir John Maffey: 'To-day', he reported in response to the news of the death of two IRA hunger strikers in Dublin, 'there was no sea of angry faces, no problem for Downing Street. *Do we realise the blessedness of this?'*[29] It was an argument MacNeice would offer an English audience in January 1941 when he had returned from America and committed, at last, to the war effort:

> I have no wish now to bring up the undying (though Chameleonic) Irish Question but I would ask you to remember that the feeling in Éire is now predominantly pro-British (though still opposed to participation in the War), that the pro-German minority is extremely small and that de Valera's position is agonisingly difficult. Those who propose the application of the strong hand to Éire are forgetting their history.[30]

Irish neutrality as an expression of the struggle to retain the ability to act independently might have been compelling, but MacNeice was aware of a less attractive strain to one aspect of neutrality: sympathy for an idealised Catholic state expressed by a relatively large degree of popular support for Franco. 'There is no room any longer for any doubts as to the issue at stake in the Spanish conflict', Cardinal Joseph MacRory, Primate of All Ireland, had told pilgrims in September 1936. 'It is a question of whether Spain will remain as she has been so long, a Christian and Catholic land, or a Bolshevist and anti-God one.'[31] A month earlier, the Irish Christian Front had been formed, declaring that 'anyone who supports the Spanish government supports church burning and priest slaughter. We should wish for the success of the Patriot arms in Spain … [because] we want the advance guard of the anti-God forces stopped in Spain.'[32]

This was a mindset that saw the war offering Éire a chance to re-set its cultural compass, as encapsulated by Francis Stuart on Germany's Redaktion-Irland radio service:

> We have had too little contact with countries that have something to give us. We have on the other hand been surrounded by communities whose life is [based] on money and the power of money …
>
> Ireland belongs to Europe and England does not belong to it. I believe that after this war our future should be linked with the future of Europe and no other.[33]

MacNeice found much to admire in de Valera's more practical admonition that neutrality was about seeking to make a place for Éire in the face of great odds and great uncertainty, a stark refutation of the grandiloquent theorising exhibited by such stalwarts of the old literary order as Walter Starkie, who in 1928 had looked forward to a

> Civilization [that would] destroy all civility and allow the individual to be free within the solidarity of the Nation. In the last five years there are not wanting signs that there is a spiritual awakening among a people that had endured years of anguish, and it is quite possible that Ireland may come to assimilate a great deal of fascist doctrine.[34]

At the outbreak of the war, MacNeice's sister was, he reported, 'seriously shocked by my schemes & thinks I should be putting my brains at the disposal of the British Government'.[35] What followed that observation was some pretty impressive intellectual callowness completely unredeemed by the final conflation of his father's religious objections to the war and his own emotional desires:

> Either European civilization is doomed or it isn't doomed. If it is doomed there is no point in prostituting my mind in its defence; if it isn't doomed I may as well be there with an unprostituted mind to carry on with it. Of course, hardly any of the English writers would agree with me … but then after all I amn't even English … but, when they tell me the situation is clear-cut, I just can't agree with them. My father fortunately thinks I am quite right.[36]

On the other hand, Nancy Sharp reported in mid-September 1939 that she had received a letter from MacNeice written 'in the utmost dejection as though he was already rotting in his grave. He seems to think that he won't revisit England. I doubt if I shall see him again for years'.[37]

MacNeice had more than war on his mind in September 1939. He had for some time been angling to get an academic appointment in the United States, or, at least, some sort of long-term lecturing opportunity, imploring T.S. Eliot to help him out. He had spent the spring of 1939 in America. He had given a few lectures and readings on the east coast and returned home in late April 1939. Just before he left, he had met Eleanor Clark at a party and had become – in customary fashion – infatuated. Their relationship would continue by correspondence until he returned to the States. In January 1940, there being no transatlantic passage from Ireland to America, MacNeice went to London, from whence he intended to travel to America. He might have been unsure about political neutrality; he had no qualms putting relationships ahead of politics.

Eliot had helped MacNeice secure a semester-long post at Cornell University with some lectures also planned, and these were bolstered by offers of additional lectures following the successful January 1940 publication of *Autumn Journal* in the United States. MacNeice enjoyed life in the States although worried about the welfare of Dan (who was living with his grandparents in Belfast until German bombing raids over that city led him first back to Cushendun and then to Dungannon, County Tyrone, before finally settling at Ashfield Lodge, in Cootehill, County Cavan, the Greer family once again proving responsive to their step-cousin's needs). His involvement with Clark, however, was fraught with tension, at least in part because of his frustration at her lack of immediate interest in a physical relationship. Those tensions were not helped by their inability to find common ground in their attitudes toward the appropriate synthesis of the cultural and the political.

Unable to gain British permission to remain in America, MacNeice chose not to renounce his British citizenship and invoke his Irish status and returned to England,[38] where he would find his friendship with Sharp on rocky ground. She had chanced upon the proofs of *The Last Ditch*, which was dedicated to Clark, while collecting some belongings from his flat. The final entry in *The Last Ditch* was 'Three Poems Apart (*For X*)'. It could not have taken Sharp long to work out the poems were for her:

>   one lies lonely, haunted
>   By limbs he half remembers,
> And one, in wedlock, wonders
>   Where is the girl he wanted.[39]

She wrote to MacNeice: 'May I ask quite simply & without tact, *why* was the poem which indeed had no possible connection with E ... included?'[40]

MacNeice now had to decide what his role would be in the war he had so far largely ignored. Life in Éire was hardly an option, unless, perhaps, he joined John Betjeman, his Marlborough contemporary, as a part of Britain's cultural mission in Dublin. There is no evidence he sought to do so. Rather, he seems to have adopted a position not dissimilar to that taken by Johnston in 1942: 'It is my belief in Ireland's neutrality that has so largely sent me forth. Only those who are prepared to go into this horrible thing themselves have the right to say that Ireland must stay out.'[41] To Clark, MacNeice observed that 'given the bloody mess that's going on, one can only get clarified through going close to it'.[42] But not returning to Éire ensured the country could remain for MacNeice both mythic and accessible by ferry.

Not long before his planned return, MacNeice was stricken by peritonitis. An emergency operation in Portsmouth, New Hampshire, saved his life but the recuperation delayed his return until late 1940. Back in Britain, it did not take long for a doctor to advise him that the after-effects of his operation meant he would likely not pass a medical board for military service, but it is possible he sought to follow his close friend Graham Shepard into the Royal Navy.[43] If so, the navy would seem to have rejected him on the grounds that his eyesight was too poor. In December 1940, MacNeice contacted Frederick Ogilvie, Director General of the BBC and the former Vice Chancellor of Queen's University, Belfast. Prior to his departure for the States, MacNeice had been taken by his sister to a London party hosted by the Ogilvies,[44] and he had noted a short while before his return that 'I just remembered the other day that the present chief of the BBC ... is a great fan of mine & a pal of the old man's, so maybe I shall cash in on that'.[45] Coincidentally, T. Rowland Hughes, the Welsh novelist integrally involved in shaping the BBC's Features and Drama department, had written to MacNeice in care of Eliot at Faber that the department was hoping 'to secure a first class poet ... [and] your lines would speak well'.[46]

While waiting to hear from the BBC, MacNeice took pen to paper and wrote a series of 'London Letters' for the American journal *Common Sense*, which was co-edited by the former brother-in-law of Clark. In his first letter, MacNeice recorded that asked to support the intention of the 'People's Convention' to revive the fortunes of the Communist Party, he had replied that 'I very much doubted (a) whether the British Communist Party could swing a revolution and (b) whether it would be the right kind of revolution'.[47] He also noted that any immediate revolution would lead 'Hitler to invade England – and probably successfully – to-morrow'.[48]

In the same letter, he outlined his practical hopes for British domestic politics and identified the crux of the problem confronting those who wished to think about the post-war settlement while focusing on winning the war:

The Labour Party ... is really more committed to winning the war than the Conservatives. It is a mistake however to hold the opinion, which I have heard expressed in America, that the Labour Party now has the whip-hand in Britain. The Labour Party is still the prisoner of the Conservatives and has to soft-pedal its own aims for fear of frightening more Conservatives into the furtive camp of Appeasement. If a general election were held to-day the Conservatives would almost certainly retain a majority ... thanks to the prestige of Churchill ... It looks as we must hope for ... Churchill to win the war and Labour to win the peace. It is a lot to hope for, but it is at least a better gamble than the other camps offer.[49]

Despite describing himself as someone 'who has never been patriotic and who loathes propaganda',[50] MacNeice joined the BBC, initially as a freelancer.[51] He took advantage of his status to note that he was 'not on the BBC but they seem prepared to employ me indefinitely. Rather preferable that way. A frightful institution to have to spend yr days in'.[52] Typically, he remained ambivalent about his commitment and returned to Éire and the north of Ireland almost immediately.

By April 1941 he was reporting that 'I have finally committed myself to supporting this war',[53] and that

I am probably going officially soon on to the staff of the BBC. It's a v. 2nd rate institution & Christ, the things they do to one's work ... but the choice of occupations here now – unless you choose to have no choice and be clapped into uniform for ever – is just a choice of evils & the BBC, though deplorable, does leave some loophole for intelligence & individual decisions.[54]

Others were less cynical, seeing the BBC as an organisation which 'in [the] face of grave doubts ... persisted obstinately in telling the truth in [its] own way'.[55] Broadcasting House resembled an ocean liner which, 'with the best engineers in the world, and a crew varying between the intensely respectable and the barely sane, looked ready to scorn any disaster of less than Titanic scale'.[56] It remained 'a cross between a civil service, a powerful moral force, and an amateur theatrical company that wasn't too sure where next week's money was coming from'.[57] By the time MacNeice arrived he found an institution unique in the contrivances of gods and men since the Oracle of Delphi. As office managers, they were no more than adequate, but now ... they were broadcasting in the strictest sense of the word, scattering human voices into the darkness of Europe, in the certainty that more than half must be lost, some for the rook, some for the crow, for the sake of a few that made their mark.[58]

MacNeice's ideas about propaganda fit comfortably with this version of how to engage in a war of words with the Axis powers. Introducing the US Army to British readers, he quoted approvingly from the American guide for troops embarking for Britain. It reminded them that 'each country has minor national characteristics which differ', and that in seeking to exploit these 'Hitler hopes to make his propaganda effective.'[59] The way to combat such intentions, he said, was not to counter with equally implausible generalisations about similarities; rather, 'you defeat enemy propaganda not by denying that these differences exist, but by admitting them openly and then trying to understand them'.[60]

Initially, MacNeice's work was primarily focused on a series of 15-minute broadcasts, 'The Stones Cry Out', aimed at telling the story of British endurance in the face of the Blitz. He would write five episodes focusing on London between May and July 1941 having already mastered the freelancer's art of repurposing work, and his early scripts for 'The Stones Cry Out' echo his 'London Letters' for *Common Sense*. He would write four more that year, including an account of the damage done to the Royal College of Surgeons, of which his brother-in-law was a fellow. In October 1941 he reported on damage inflicted on Belfast, which would be the last time he saw his father in good health. The following month he reported on damage to Plymouth, a location he seems to have chosen, at least in part, because his sister was working there. Proximity to his family aside, MacNeice had quickly adopted the BBC's 'actuality' ethos that required even scripted work to have as significant a degree of local authenticity as possible in its recording.

The success in America of *Autumn Journal* encouraged Random House to issue a volume of his work in late 1940. Blurbed on the dust jacket as 'The collected poetry of one of the leaders among England's younger generation of poets', it was not exactly a 'collected' edition, but it was too extensive to be accurately described as a 'selected' volume. MacNeice supplied a brief foreword in which he suggested that 'I am not collecting [my poetry] because I am dead, but because my past life is. Like most other people in the British Isles I have little idea what will happen next.'[61]

The first volume of that new life was published in April 1941. Much of *Plant and Phantom* had appeared, sometimes in a different form and often in a different order, in *The Last Ditch*; tellingly, MacNeice retained for the heavily revised version of 'The Coming of War' the title he had adopted for the Random House collection, 'The Closing Album'.

In September 1940, MacNeice had written to Eliot providing a list of poems he wanted to see in *Plant and Phantom*. He added brief annotation as to whether they had been written in America, had appeared in *The Last Ditch*, were 'connected with the war' and the date on which they had been finished.[62] One poem not on that list was 'Plain Speaking'. It had appeared as 'The Undeniable Fact' in *Poems 1925–1940*, dated March 1940. Why MacNeice omitted it from the proposed list he sent Eliot is not clear, but Eliot's hand in the version of *Plant and Phantom* as published is apparent, and he, presumably, found in the re-titled poem something worth convincing MacNeice to include. It's not hard to see why:

> In the beginning and in the end the only decent
> Definition is tautology: man is man,
> Woman woman, and tree tree, and world world,
> Slippery, self-contained; catch as catch can.[63]

This was the world MacNeice intended to preserve and catch as he could, even if there happened to be a war raging around him. And in the poem which precedes 'Plain Speaking', 'Plurality', the argument is fleshed out:

> And, if we use the world Eternal, stake a claim
> Only to what a bird can find within the frame
> Of momentary flight (the value will persist
> But as event the night sweeps it away in mist).
> Man is man because he might have been a beast.[64]

There might have been a war on, but family connections continued to enable MacNeice to live a relatively unencumbered life. He moved in mid-1941 into Byron Cottage in Highgate, on the edge of Hampstead Heath, where A.E. Housman had written *A Shropshire Lad* and which was then owned by John and Elizabeth Nicholson. While there, Louis posed for the photographer Bill Brandt, whose portraits accompany Stephen Spender's late 1941 consideration of 'Young Poets of Democracy'. He depicted MacNeice comfortably settled in one of the Nicholsons's armchairs by a window with sun lighting the warm room, a poet very much at peace with himself and the world.[65]

In December 1941, his programme about Alexander Nevsky's 1242 defeat of an invading Teutonic army was abruptly pre-empted for a story from the other side of the world: Japanese planes had bombed Pearl Harbor. MacNeice's experience in America and his increasing fluency with the language of radio made him an obvious central creative figure as the BBC shifted its focus from strengthening resolve on the home front to ensuring a welcome for American forces. In October 1942, MacNeice's *Christopher Columbus* was broadcast on the Home Service of the BBC to mark the 300th anniversary of Columbus's journey west. It is a radio drama that in many ways is the first fully-fledged expression of the aesthetic and moral endeavours that would inform MacNeice's work going forward.

Christopher Columbus was published in 1944 and MacNeice took the opportunity to write an introduction that serves as an essay on his understanding of sound: 'A good radio play … presupposes a good radio script [and] such a script is not necessarily a piece of "good writing".'[66] Radio offered the opportunity to balance the commonplace and the poetic, for

> provided his piece is well produced, [the writer] can count on his words regaining those literary virtues which literature itself has lost since it has been divorced from the voice … With a literature so old as ours and a contemporary diction so vulgarised, precise and emotive writing comes to depend more and more upon twists – twists of the obvious statement or the hackneyed image. To do this on the printed page requires constant ingenuity and often leads to an appearance of being too clever by half. In radio … you can leave the twisting to the voices.[67]

The writer, of course, is not alone, and MacNeice grapples, as he had earlier with his thoughts on stage drama, with the relationship between author and audience, worrying that the trouble with 'ordinary people' is not that they have innately bad taste but that they can be easily taught to admire what is vulgar and emotionally false. Give them a year of the Wurlitzer Organ and they will not stomach a symphony orchestra. Write down to them and they will never look up.[68]

Christopher Columbus might have been 'written to order and with a special end in view',[69] but MacNeice managed nonetheless to create a play about the struggle between conviction and doubts, about faith over logic, or, rather, about faith *as* logic. He also worked in his own reservations about national identity. Defined as a 'citizen of Genoa' by the chair of the tribunal summoned to weigh the merits of his plan, Columbus objects: 'I am *not* a citizen of Genoa'.[70] Told 'A man must have some country', he answers that 'My country, my Lord, is the Future'.[71] Indeed, only in the very conclusion of Columbus's final speech does MacNeice address the charge given to him by those commissioning the play, when Columbus says of the land he has found, 'God alone knows what it will become | Or what may be the blessings that late or soon | May flow from thence to Europe'.[72]

One advantage of working for the BBC was the proximity to many artists and performers, and toward the end of 1941 MacNeice re-encountered Hedli Anderson, whom he had first met at a 1934 Group Theatre production of Auden's *The Dance of Death*. When she saw him at a party in London he looked, even for him, particularly lonesome. She made a point of talking to him. In typical fashion, he quickly decided he was irretrievably in love, and on his return from Belfast and Cootehill after the death of his father and a visit to Dan, they decided to get married, at least in part, if his letter announcing the fact to Sharp is to be believed, because they 'got fed up with the inconveniences of our status' as it affected her ability to accompany him on trips to Éire and to Belfast.[73] At the time of his marriage, Sharp was involved in divorcing her husband and marrying Michael Spender, Stephen's older brother. In 1940, she had joined the London Auxiliary Ambulance Service, driving through London during the Blitz 'erratically and eccentrically, but with great courage'.[74] MacNeice's marriage would not, he promised Sharp, 'change anything between you and me'.[75] More breathtakingly, he wrote a quick letter to Clark telling her the news 'that I have got married – but not to anyone I had mentioned to you before'.[76]

MacNeice continued to find the war less a compelling cause than an experience not to be missed. But then it all got very personal. Graham Shepard died when HMS *Polyanthus* was torpedoed on 20 September 1943, en route to Newfoundland. From the start of the war there had been speculation that U-boats were secretly using Irish coves and small ports for refuelling, albeit that there was both no evidence of this and an active Irish Coast Watch designed to prevent such activity. MacNeice's support of Éire's right to neutrality did not prevent him turning his ire once more on the island of his birth. His shock by one loss in the midst of so many had suddenly brought the war home to him. His sympathy for the idea of Irish neutrality remained: 'Look into your heart, you will find a County Sligo, | A Knocknarea with for navel a cairn of stones'

> Look into your heart, you will find fermenting rivers,
> Intricacies of gloom and glint,
> You will find such ducats of dream and great doubloons of ceremony
> As nobody to-day would mint.[77]

But now, too, he demanded the Irish

> look east from your heart, there bulks
> A continent, close, dark, as archetypal sin,
> While to the west off your own shores the mackerel
> Are fat – on the flesh of your kin.[78]

The war and the death of his father, marriage, the death of a friend and the birth of a daughter, Corinna, shaped MacNeice's renewed conviction in the value of the human moment. He carried forward, too, his ambivalence about neutrality. Éire might have asserted its rightful claim to manage its own affairs, but a broader cause was being fought at least in part to defend the rights it had used to abstain from that fight. In response, MacNeice would turn away from the urge to make something from the literal rubble of the war, reject the planning and schemes that would reshape society and would choose to sing instead the song of 'The incorruptible souls who work without a commission'.[79] Henceforward, he would praise those 'humble | And proud at once, working within their limits | And yet transcending them', those 'Loyal by intuition, born to attack, and innocent'.[80]

NOTES

References to the poems of Louis MacNeice are as they appear in Peter McDonald (ed.), *Collected Poems* (London: Faber, 2007), except as noted.

1   Louis MacNeice, 'To Eleanor Clark', p.678.
2   Louis MacNeice, 'The Coming of War (*Dublin, Cushendun, the West of Ireland, and back*)', I, 'Dublin', pp.680–6 (p.680).
3   Ibid., p.680.
4   Ibid., II, p.682.
5   Ibid., V, p.683.
6   Jon Stallworthy, *Louis MacNeice* (London: Faber, 1995), p.259.
7   Louis MacNeice, *The Strings Are False: An Unfinished Autobiography*, ed. E.R. Dodds (London: Faber, 1965), p.212.
8   Clair Wills, *That Neutral Island: A Cultural History of Ireland during the Second World War* (London: Faber, 2007), p.75.
9   MacNeice, *Strings*, p.213.
10 Elizabeth Bowen, 'Notes on Éire' [9 November 1940], [PRO DO 800/310], in Jack Lane and Brendan Clifford (eds),'*Notes on Éire*', *Espionage Reports to Winston Churchill, 1940–2: With a Review of Irish Neutrality in World War II* (Millstreet: Aubane Historical Society, 1999), p.12.
11 Clair Wills, 'The Aesthetics of Irish Neutrality during the Second World War', *boundary2*, 31:1 (spring 2004), pp.119–145 (p.121).
12 Antoinette Quinn, *Patrick Kavanagh: A Biography* (Dublin: Gill and Macmillan, 2003), p.127.
13 Ibid.
14 Ibid.
15 Louis MacNeice to Eleanor Clark, 8 May [1939], p.357.
16 'A Literary Night Out', produced by Roibeárd Ó Faracháin, Radio Éireann, 12 October 1939.
17 Roibeárd Ó Faracháin, 'Some Early Days in Radio', in Louis McRedmond (ed.),*Written on the Wind: Personal Memories of Irish Radio* (Dublin: Raidió Teilifís Éireann, 1976), pp.29–50 (p.40).
18 Patrick Kavanagh, 'The Great Hunger', produced by Louis MacNeice, BBC Radio Third Programme, 13 May 1960. It must have been an interesting experience as the *Radio Times* reported that 'This long poem tells the story of a farmer in County Monaghan. Though it caused a stir when it was first published in 1947, the poet no longer likes it', *Radio Times*, 1904 (6 May 1960), p.47.
19 Cited in Brian Fallon, 'F.R. Higgins: A Neglected Master Craftsman', *The Irish Times*, 8 January 1991, p.8.
20 'Tendencies in Modern Poetry', BBC Northern Ireland, 11 July 1939; printed as F.R. Higgins and Louis MacNeice, 'Tendencies in Modern Poetry', *The Listener*, 22:550 (27 July 1939), pp.185–6 (p.185).
21 Ibid., p.186.

22   Ibid., See also, Tom Walker, 'MacNeice among his Irish Contemporaries: 1939 and 1945', in Fran Brearton andAlan Gillis (eds),*The Oxford Handbook of Modern Irish Poetry* (Oxford: Oxford University Press, 2012), pp.196–209 (pp.198–9).

23   Louis MacNeice, *Autumn Sequel*, XVIII, p.455.

24   Denis Johnston, 'Dionysia: an Account of the Author's Experiences as a BBC War Correspondent, 1942–45', typescript, British Library; qtd in Wills, 'The Aesthetics of Irish Neutrality', p.129.

25   Kate O'Brien, *The Last of Summer* (London: Heinemann, 1943), p.81.

26   Joseph Walsh to John Hearne, 26 February 1940, in Catriona Crowe, Ronan Fanning, Michael Kennedy, Eunan O'Halpin and Dermot Keogh (eds), *Documents on Irish Foreign Policy* Volume VI, *1939–1941* (Dublin: Royal Irish Academy, 2008), p.156.

27   Hearne to Walsh, 27 June 1940, in ibid., p.267. Given the complaints of Irish diplomats abroad about the difficulty they had in receiving news from Éire, Hearne was likely drawing on the report in *Time* magazine that mentioned the 'enormous support of the Catholic Church' toward Irish neutrality provided by the bishop's remarks. Éire was, wrote *Time*'s anonymous correspondent, 'neutral against everyone' ['Éire: Against Everybody?' *Time*, 35:24 (10 June 1940), p.38].

28   Bowen, 'Notes on Éire' [9 November 1940], p.12.

29   Sir John Maffey to Dominion Office, 22 April 1940, [PRO DO 130/12]. See also, Brian Girvin, *The Emergency: Neutral Ireland 1939–45* (London: Macmillan, 2006), p.97. [Italics in the original.]

30   Louis MacNeice, 'London Letter [3]: War Aims; the New Political Alignment', in *Common Sense*, 10:5 (May 1941), pp.142–3; repr. in Alan Heuser (ed.), *Selected Prose of Louis MacNeice* (Oxford: Oxford University Press, 1990), pp.112–116 (p.116).

31   Qtd in Sean Cronin, *Frank Ryan – The Search for The Republic* (Dublin: Repsol, 1980), p.79.

32   Manifesto of the Irish Christian Front, 1936; qtd in Peter Manifold, 'Irish Responses to the Outbreak of the Spanish Civil War: A Comparative Approach to the Study of Irish Foreign Policy', unpub. PhD Diss., Dublin City University, Dublin, 2012, p.41.

33   Francis Stuart, Broadcast of 17 March 1942 on Redaktion-Irland [Directorate of Intelligence (G2) transcription], in Brendan Barrington (ed.), *The Wartime Broadcasts of Francis Stuart, 1942–1944* (Dublin: Lilliput, 2001), pp.69–70 (p.70).

34   Walter Starkie, 'Whither is Ireland Heading – Is it Fascism? Thoughts on the Irish Free State', in *Survey of Fascism Year Book* (Lausanne: International Fascist Organisation; London: Ernest Benn, 1928), pp.223–34; qtd in Wills, *That Neutral Island*, p.348. [Aspirationally sub-titled vol. 1; no further volumes appeared.]

35   Louis MacNeice to Eleanor Clark, 24 September [1939], p.357.

36   Ibid.

37   Nancy Sharp to John Auden, 13 September 1939. The letter is in private hands.

38   The US State Department extended MacNeice's work permit for twelve months, but the British government refused to grant an extension to his exit visa from Britain. MacNeice could, in theory, have used his now explicit Irish citizenship to claim he was not subject to

that recall, but travel to Éire was, by necessity, through Britain – neutral non-Irish ships generally avoided Irish ports as there was no Irish navy to escort them and Germany had declared the approaches to Éire legitimate war zones as those approaches also served British ports. For details of the Irish merchant marine during the Second World War, see, Frank Forde, *'The Long Watch': The History of the Irish Mercantile Marine in World War Two* (Dublin: Gill and Macmillan, 1981).

39	Louis MacNeice, 'Three Poems Apart *(for X)*', I, pp.697–8 (p.697).

40	Nancy Sharp to Louis MacNeice, 10 February 1940; qtd in *MacNeice*, p.278. [Italics in the original.]

41	Qtd in Bernard Adams, *Denis Johnston: A Life* (Dublin: Lilliput, 2002), p.216.

42	Louis MacNeice to Eleanor Clark, [10 October 1940], p.411.

43	Stallworthy, *Louis MacNeice*, p.287.

44	Barbara Coulton, *Louis MacNeice in the BBC* (London: Faber, 1980), p.46.

45	Louis MacNeice to Mary Katzman [Ezra], 28 October 1940, p.414.

46	T. Rowland Hughes to Louis MacNeice, 7 March 1940; qtd in *MacNeice*, p.287.

47	Louis MacNeice, 'London Letter [1]: Blackouts, Bureaucracy & Courage', *Common Sense*, 10:2 (February 1941), pp.46–7; repr. in *Selected Prose*, pp.99–105 (p.103).

48	Ibid.

49	Ibid., p.104.

50	Ibid.

51	Ibid.

52	Louis MacNeice to E.R. Dodds, 10 February [1941], p.421.

53	Same to same, 3 April [1941], p.427.

54	Same to same, 20 April [1941], p.429.

55	Penelope Fitzgerald, *Human Voices* (London: Flamingo, 1988), p.35.

56	Ibid., pp.10–11.

57	Ibid., p.35.

58	Ibid., p.77. There are two references in this passage MacNeice would have immediately recognised in the words of Penelope Fitzgerald, his contemporary at the BBC. The metaphor draws on Jesus's parable of the sower, Matt. 13:1-23. The phrase 'human voices' echoes the last line of T.S. Eliot's poem 'The Love Song of J. Alfred Prufrock': 'Till human voices wake us, and we drown' [*Prufrock and Other Observations* (London: The Egoist, 1917), pp.9–16 (p.16)].

59	Louis MacNeice, *Meet the U.S. Army* (London: HMSO, 1943), p.6, quoting *Instructions for American Servicemen in Britain* (Washington, D.C.: War Department, 1942), p.2.

60	Ibid.

61	Louis MacNeice, 'Foreword', in *Poems 1925–1940* (New York, NY: Random House, 1940), pp.xiii–xiv (p.xiii).

62	Louis MacNeice to T.S. Eliot, 24 September 1940, pp.408–10.

63	Louis MacNeice, 'Plain Speaking', p.206.

64	Louis MacNeice, 'Plurality', pp.204-6 (p.205).

65	Stephen Spender, 'Poetry and the English', *Lilliput*, 9:6 (December 1941), pp.477–84.

66	Louis MacNeice 'Introduction', in *Christopher Columbus: A Radio Play* (London: Faber, 1944), pp.7–19 (p.7).

67 Ibid., pp.8–9.

68 Ibid., pp.9–10.

69 MacNeice, *Christopher Columbus*, Appendix, p.88.

70 Ibid, p.42. [Italics in the original.]

71 Ibid.

72 Ibid., p.86.

73 Louis MacNeice to Nancy Sharp, [2 July 1942], p.444.

74 John Margetson, 'Nancy Spender' (Obituary), *The Guardian*, 25 June 2001,<http://www.theguardian.com/news/2001/jun/25/guardianobituaries.arts>, accessed 17 June 2015. Her account of the first night of the Blitz, 7 September 1940, and its devastating effect in Silvertown, West Ham, can be found in Constantine FitzGibbon, *The Blitz* (London: Wingate, 1957), pp.67–70. She can also be heard recounting her experiences on FitzGibbon's 'The Winter of the Bombs', BBC Home Service, Sunday 29 September, 1957. Produced by FitzGibbon and Robert Pocock.

75 Louis MacNeice to Nancy Sharp, [2 July 1942]; qtd in *MacNeice*, p.310.

76 Louis MacNeice to Eleanor Clark, [9 July 1942], p.445.

77 Louis MacNeice, 'Neutrality', p.224.

78 Ibid.

79 Louis MacNeice, 'The Kingdom', pp.241–9 (I, p.241).

80 Ibid., p.242.

CHAPTER 8

Surviving the Peace

Louis MacNeice was no more a 'war' poet than he had been a 'political' poet in the 1930s. In many ways the war merely intensified his conviction about the necessity of proclaiming the value of individual human expression in the face of broader political and social demands. His was a position sympathetic to T.S. Eliot's identification of the 'dissociation of sensibility' as the essential modern condition, albeit with one profoundly different component. Eliot had identified in the Metaphysical poets writers whose world splintered around them.[1] For Eliot, their struggle to restore order and meaning was a profoundly modern dilemma. 'The Waste Land' and Four Quartets, in particular, had demonstrated his response to this challenge.[2] They are poems redolent with the awful recognition that 'if we make our own meanings God will oblige us to answer our own questions. He will leave us in the void without the comfort of His Word'.[3] Recognising the same looming void as Eliot and the Metaphysical poets but lacking God to provide meaning, MacNeice looked to individual integrity to 'Patch up our broken hearts' in the face of 'Those who shall supersede us and cannot need us – | Those tight-lipped technocratic Conquistadores'.[4]

For 'Prayer before Birth', the opening poem of Springboard, the only volume of his composed exclusively of wartime poems, MacNeice explicitly turned for a model to the Metaphysical poet whose work most seamlessly integrates the human and the eternal – George Herbert, Anglican divine and poet of meticulous craft and spiritual sensuousness. For Herbert, all of life was an opportunity for the human spirit to witness the divinity of creation. His poems are thus both intensely physical and openly spiritual, cousin to, but distinct from, the poetry of John Donne, whom he knew well and whose patron was Herbert's mother. MacNeice recognised in Herbert a poet who was a master of praising the specific, valuing the moment and finding in it intimations of immortality. For Herbert, as for MacNeice's father, those intimations of immortality were evidence of God's grace. For MacNeice, they were the reason to claim a human delight in the face of the increasingly systemic.

'Prayer before Birth' opens with an epigraph from Herbert's 'Providence' – 'Ev'n poisons praise thee' – a poem of joyous celebration of the evidence of God's love.[5] But MacNeice found the structure for 'Prayer before Birth', and the theme for the volume as a whole, in another of Herbert's poems, 'Sighs and Grones'. Herbert's poem is a plea for God's grace. The opening stanza sets the tone:

> O Do not use me
> After my sinnes! Look not on my desert,
> But on thy glorie! Then thou wilt reform
> And not refuse me: for thou onely art
> The mightie God, but I a sillie worm.
> O do not bruise me![6]

Without God to appeal to, MacNeice's poem seeks, instead of grace, protection, but who might provide that is unclear. It is a poem not of supplication but of determination to try to remain an individual in the face of what might come:

> I am not yet born, console me.
> I fear that the human race may with tall walls wall me,
>   with strong drugs dope me, with wise lies lure me,
>   on black racks rack me, in blood-baths roll me.[7]

Both Herbert's poem and MacNeice's echo Job's lament:

> Let the day perish wherein I was born, and the night in which it was
>   said, There is a man child conceived.
> Let that day be darkness; let not God regard it from above, neither let
>   the light shine up on it.

> Let darkness and the shadow of death stain it; let a cloud dwell upon
>   it; let the blackness of the day terrify it.
> As for that night, let darkness seize upon it; let it not be joined
>   unto the days of the year, let it not come into the number of the
>   months.[8]

MacNeice and Herbert both would have known the bleakness of the
conclusion of Job's lament: 'I was not in safety, neither had I rest, neither
was I quiet; yet trouble came.'[9] It was a lament Herbert's faith in the God
of the New Testament quieted but to which MacNeice's scepticism never
quite provided a balm.

Reviewing Aldous Huxley's later prose four years after the publication
of *Springboard*, MacNeice would observe that 'it's high time to remember
the soul but, whatever that entity is, it's surely not smug? And, if you're
preaching the gospel of love, need you look down your nose all the time?'[10]
How to cherish the 'soul' would increasingly form the core of MacNeice's
creative work, a response to the knowledge that for each of us there would
be 'sins that in me the world shall commit', and 'treason engendered by
traitors beyond me' and 'murder by means of my | hands'.[11] The poems of
this period turn inwards, private concerns about personal integrity in the
face of

> those who would freeze my
> humanity, would dragoon me into a lethal automaton,
>   would make me a cog in a machine, a thing with
>   one face, a thing.[12]

While one might expect to find such sentiments accompanied by an
almost all-encompassing cynicism, MacNeice refused to discount the
human potential, and he could affirm without irony that 'the fact I think
every institution and dogma – and nearly every person – need mocking
has not made me a cynic.'[13]

One of those few exempt from the need for scrutiny was MacNeice's
old friend Graham Shepard, eulogised in the opening poem of the short
second section of *Springboard*. 'The Casualty' is a heartfelt tribute to one
than 'whom I do not expect ever again | To find a more accordant friend'.[14]
Unlike MacNeice, Shepard was 'a good mixer and could laugh | With
Rowlandson or Goya'.[15] Like Nancy Sharp, he was

Creative not for the counter or the shelf
But innocently whom the world bewilders
And so they observe it and love it till their mind
May turn them from mere students into builders.[16]

Shepard offered those most valuable of insights, 'inklings: trivial signs | Of some momentous truth'.[17] His gift was that he was 'Surprised and therefore sympathetic, warm | Towards things as well as people'.[18] His memory offered MacNeice the strength to 'hope that fact is a façade | And that there is an organism behind | Its brittle littleness',[19] to search for 'Something half-conjectured and half-divined, | Something to give way to and so find'.[20]

Much of the strength of *Springboard* lies in its acknowledgment of the interior struggle, in the knowledge that

                      it was more than fright
That kept him crucified among the budding stars.

Yes, it was unbelief. He knew only too well
That circumstances called for sacrifice
But, shivering there, spreadeagled above the town,
His blood began to haggle over the price.[21]

Crucially, MacNeice held that 'unbelief' can substitute for 'belief', although he stressed that 'unbelief' is not simply 'belief' with no positive expression.[22] The price being haggled over reveals the full extent of the task facing those whose unbelief would be positive: 'If it would mend the world, that would be worth while | But he, quite rightly, long had ceased to believe | in any Utopia.'[23]

MacNeice was not moving any closer to the religion of his father; he never would. But he came increasingly to see how his father's integrity of purpose had created a life that was itself of a piece, and he wondered how to recognise that integrity in others and how to shape it in himself. The bishop's comments on broad social developments foreshadowed his son's analysis. 'Life has become harder and more drab and more meaningless for far too many of our people; this problem, fundamentally moral and spiritual, presses for solution', the bishop had said in his 1935 Christmas letter.[24] 'The Kingdom', the long poem that all but concludes *Springboard*, demonstrates the strengths and weaknesses of MacNeice's commitment to praise those who would make meaning in the face of the drab and cherish the individual whatever the attraction of the group. Showing its debt to rhetorical strategies MacNeice had developed at the BBC, 'The Kingdom' opens with an exposition of the general point that will be illustrated by the specific examples which follow, much as the various episodes of 'The Stones Cry Out' began with an exhortatory reason to listen. The result is that the first section is better as a framing device than as poetry, with its call to 'Go wherever you choose, among tidy villas or terrible | Docks, dumps and pitheads, or through the spangled moors',[25] to meet those 'Apart from those who drift and those who force, | Apart from partisan order and egotistical anarchy',[26] those who 'working within their limits' nonetheless 'transcend them'.[27]

The portraits which follow are most vital when they are of real people. Such is the case with the second section, another account of MacNeice's headmaster at Sherborne Prep, Littleton Powys, which includes perhaps MacNeice's most perfect poetic sentence: 'Through serene and chequered | Fields that he knows he walks like a fallen angel | Whose fall has made him a man.'[28] The absence of any guiding commas offers multiple meanings simultaneously within the reference to a biblical story MacNeice found inspiring in Milton's re-telling precisely because of its outcome – Adam and Eve walking out into the world hand in hand, aware, at last, of the importance of that simple human gesture.

The heart of 'The Kingdom', however, is its penultimate section, a report of his father's funeral service constructed with an eye on the poetry, an ear on the sound and a mind on the lesson, and absolute proof, if proof were still needed, that the poet of the 1930s had learned well from the radio dramatist of the 1940s:

All is well, said the voice from the tiny pulpit,[29]
All is well with the child. And the voice cracked
For the preacher was very old and the coffin down in the aisle
Held the body of one who had been his friend and colleague
For forty years and was dead in daffodil time
Before it had come to Easter. All is well with
One who believed and practised and whose life
Presumed the Resurrection. What that means
He may have felt he knew; this much is certain –
The meaning filled his actions, made him courteous

And lyrical and strong and kind and truthful,
A generous puritan.[30]

Before VE day but with victory certain, MacNeice and Anderson once again travelled to Northern Ireland to stay with his stepmother, now back in Carrickfergus and living at Oakfield House,[31] but they spent more time in Éire, this time in Achill, County Mayo, no longer obliged to make Belfast the centre of his Irish trips. MacNeice must have travelled to Belfast at least once during that time, however, and the Glasgow-born but very much Ulster-based novelist Sam Hanna Bell recalled that he, MacNeice and W.R. 'Bertie' Rodgers were in a Belfast pub when news came of the August 6 bombing of Hiroshima.[32] MacNeice spent several months in Éire despite having no leave from the BBC. He invoked, once again, his 'Irishness', justifying his actions by stating that 'I am … Irish & have not been in my own country for 3 years – and not for so long then.'[33] This assertion of Irishness did not mean MacNeice was any more comfortable with the island than he had traditionally been, and in a note to the published version of the 1946 radio drama 'Salute to All Fools' commenting on the Dáil's language laws his ambivalence was on display: 'Let me say that I dissociate the language lunacy from the question of Éire's independence; I am glad that she runs her own house but why need she keep the windows shut?'[34]

In November 1945, he again returned to Belfast to produce for BBC Northern Ireland the first of Rodgers's radio scripts, *The City Set on a Hill*. Rodgers was a Presbyterian minister, and both he and MacNeice, along with many of their listeners, would have got both the biblical reference and the specific description of the city of Armagh with its twin cathedrals on the top of twin hills.[35] MacNeice also offered a poem, a delightful paean to a godfather, to the fourth issue of *Lagan*, a literary journal committed to promoting the literature 'springing out of the life and speech of this province', founded by Bell, John Hewitt and John Boyd.[36] Boyd's introductory comments to the issue begin with the observation that '*Lagan* has survived the war: and the problem now is to survive the peace.'[37] It did not. Éire, Northern Ireland, England: by the end of the war MacNeice claimed any and all as his birthright, moving between them unable to find one to call home for sure. 'Surviving the peace' amidst so much dislocation would be the focus of MacNeice's work for the next few years. The continuous act of commitment required for that survival was on full display in the radio drama *The Dark Tower*, essentially finished while he was in Achill. The play was suggested by Robert Browning's poem 'Childe Roland to the Dark Tower Came', whose conclusion MacNeice parses to stress that 'Roland did not have to – he did not wish to – and yet in the end he came to: The Dark Tower.'[38] The poem had the additional advantage of 'not admit[ting] of a completely rational analysis and still less add[ing] up to any clear moral or message'.[39]

Tantalisingly, throughout much of the play there is an alternative available to Roland in the form of Sylvie, who offers him 'the gift of common sense',[40] who cautions him that

> Those who have power
> Are mad enough but there *are* people, Roland,
> Who keep themselves to themselves or rather to each other,
> Living a sane and gentle life in a forest nook or a hill pocket,
> Perpetuating their kind and their kindness, keeping
> Their hands clean and their eyes keen, at one with
> Themselves, each other and nature.[41]

Her advocacy of keeping oneself to oneself evokes the most optimistic Irish argument for Irish neutrality in the just concluded war. Sylvie and Roland's relationship mirrors, too, the choice that those with dual allegiances had had to make. Like MacNeice, Roland took his time between the initial summons and finally committing to the quest, diverted en route by hopes for an alternative idyll.

Ultimately, Roland's rejection of Sylvie's position is more problematic than redemptive, and it is not until he has no choice at the very end that he is finally roused to claim irrevocably that what he does next – sounding the challenge that will summon the dragon and, presumably, lead to his death – he does in the name of free will. The rejection of the idyll, 'your little house and your apple orchard' where Sylvie will 'marry one of your own kind | And spray the trees in spring and raise the ladders in autumn | And spread the shining crop on the spare-room floor',[42] is at odds with the connection to nature for which MacNeice had praised Littleton Powys in both *Autumn Journal* and 'The Kingdom', and which he would recognise again in Powys's 'lasting love for worlds that are wide and green | Through which, through Arthur's land, he walks a prince';[43] but it is also a refutation of the idea that in post-war Britain such dreams are still meaningful. MacNeice's poetry and his drama had turned darker and the pity starker.

The poetry of *Springboard* and the drama of *The Dark Tower* share the awareness that actions take place in time even as their justification must be independent of that temporality. It was a dichotomy MacNeice had touched on earlier, most eloquently in his 'Letter to Graham and Anne Shepard'. He had gone to Iceland, he had told them, because he had 'nothing better to do. | But all the same we never make any choice | On such a merely mechanical stimulus'.[44] Similarly to MacNeice's explorations in *Springboard* and *The Dark Tower*, Auden's 1947 *The Age of Anxiety: A Baroque Eclogue* tackled these questions in a book-length poem in which he solved the problem of what sort of verse to use 'by inventing an alliterative line, reminiscent in some ways of the sagas … The insistence on three alliterative words per line is never relaxed, and it is only through his enormous technical skill that the whole performance is bearable'.[45] The latter part of this observation is a charge that would later be laid at MacNeice's door when he published *Autumn Sequel*.

Auden's title alluded to Søren Kierkegaard's 1844 exploration of *The Concept of Anxiety*.[46] MacNeice shared with Auden and Kierkegaard, while rejecting their Christianity, a sense that anxiety must accompany any choice worth making, for

> on one side is the dread burden of choosing for eternity; on the other side is the exhilaration of freedom in choosing oneself. Choice occurs in the … point at which time and eternity intersect – for the individual creates through temporal choice a self which will be judged for eternity.[47]

MacNeice also shared with Kierkegaard a sense of the eternal inherent in the constant repetition of life, whether it be accidental, as in the roses out of time but not out of place on the windowsill in 'Snow', or deliberate, as in the choice Roland repeatedly makes to reject the possibilities suggested by Sylvie and, in doing so, to assert the integrity of his future self, his present promise and his past decisions.[48] An awareness of anxiety and repetition increasingly informs MacNeice's post-war works. 'Been here before? Whether he has or no, | The question is: Must he be here for ever?' he asks at the opening to Canto XV of *Autumn Sequel*.[49] It was a question of increasing import to MacNeice as he moved from youth through middle age toward the old age he never saw.

Holes in the Sky followed *Springboard* in 1948, a reflection on 'The years that did not count – Civilians in the towns | Remained the same age as in Nineteen-Thirty-Nine, | Saying last year, meaning the last year of peace'.[50] In Ireland as the war ended, MacNeice had returned to Carrickfergus where 'memories ... peer[ed] ... from the shelf', reaffirming his conviction that 'Our past we know | But not its meaning – whether it meant well'.[51] He recalled a visit with his father to the Strand at Achill, a man who

> for all his responsibly compiled
> Account books of a devout, precise routine
> Kept something about him solitary and wild,
>
> So loved the western sea and no tree's green
> Fulfilled him like these contours of Slievemore
> Menaun and Croaghaun and the bogs between.[52]

He found, too, 'the English landscape tame' while for his son the English woods teemed with 'Malory's knights, | Keats's nymphs or the Midsummer Night's Dream',[53] but his father was 'maybe right' for the English woods are 'not the Forest; each is moored | To a village somewhere near'.[54] 'They are not like the wilds of Mayo' and 'always we walk out again'.[55]

There was now for MacNeice both a permanent divide between potential and actual and an undeniable connection, so that

> Suspended in a moving night
> The face in the reflected train
> Looks at first sight as self-assured
> As your own face – But look again:
>
> Windows between you and the world
> Keep out the cold, keep out the fright;
> Then why does your reflection seem
> So lonely in the moving night?[56]

And in another poem that relies upon a train for its setting, he considers 'the girl opposite' who is 'Asleep and the colour of her eyes unknown | Which might be wells of sun or moons of wish', but if the girl were to 'open her eyes' she would 'so doing, open ours' and in so doing might just reinvigorate the poet on his journey.[57] Aware of the potential, there is little he can do to act upon it save wait for it to find him.

Holes in the Sky concludes with a long, unsuccessfully didactic poem. 'The Stygian Banks' was the clearest warning yet that when MacNeice let go of real people and real places in his poems he tended also to lose the voice that gave a reason to his always impressive technical prowess. It is a poem that seeks to make sense of the implications that

> It is your birthright never to be grown up
> But always growing, never yourself completed
> As are the brutes, and therefore, unlike the brutes,
> Able to shape something outside yourself
> Finding completion only in otherness.[58]

'Otherness' was something MacNeice was increasingly exposed to. The BBC sent him to India in 1947 to report on events leading up to independence and partition, and the resulting programmes are a testament to his attention to sound and sight, to the colours and the noise, the heat and the light of that vast, teeming sub-continent.

Back in England, he had grown restless and took a leave from the BBC in 1950 and 1951 to serve as director of the British Institute in Athens, which would merge while he was there with the British Council. He and Anderson entertained the Greek intelligentsia, performed what would become a staple double act of her songs and his poetry, including songs he wrote for her, and generally spent a year never quite getting to grips with the country. The volume that followed, *Ten Burnt Offerings*, owed its title to the classical Greek tradition MacNeice knew so well and drew upon Psalm 66 and its promise that 'I will go into thy house with burnt offerings: I will pay thee my vows.'[59]

The ten poems were 'more architectural – or perhaps I should say symphonic – than what I was doing before'.[60] Although not initially written with radio in mind, MacNeice soon decided they were suitable for broadcast and the BBC Third Programme aired them between September and November 1951, produced by Terence Tiller. It might seem unnecessary to stress the importance of sound in poetry, but *Ten Burnt Offerings* and its successor, *Autumn Sequel*, are not poems to be read so much as they are poems to be heard, sustained sequences building a soundscape. Just as it is possible to excerpt passages from Edmund Spenser's epic *The Faerie Queene* to give the reader a sense of the whole but hard to provide excerpts that are themselves self-contained and fully formed, so the same is true of both *Ten Burnt Offerings* and *Autumn Sequel*. The ten entries in *Ten Burnt Offerings* are individual poems, but read as a whole they gain a layer of cohesion and the volume perfectly embodies Ferdinand Brunetière's definition of 'classique', that the whole is greater than the sum of the parts.[61] That said, MacNeice had enough confidence in the poems individually that for his 1959 collection *Eighty-Five Poems* he omitted all but two of them, 'Didymus' and 'Day of Returning', a poem 'counterpointing Odysseus and Jacob, "both 'practical' men"'.[62]

Indeed, however strong the collection as a whole, the volume is surely worth its place on any bookshelf for the poem that grapples with the most startling existential quandary of them all: Doubting Thomas's unique position as the only follower of Christ who could not *believe* because he *knew*, the terrible fate of the man who had thrust his fingers into the wounds of Christ because he wanted certainty over faith. How to respond in time to that eternal failure, how to redeem that temporal failure in eternity, was a question MacNeice grasped head-on in a poem that, inter alia, demonstrates a remarkable sensory wall of sound and sight developed far beyond that seen in earlier poems, such as 'Birmingham', that also sought to evoke a mood through cataloguing the individual components of a place.

'Didymus' opens by summoning sight and sound and mood, positioning the reader immediately:

A million shimmering kettles: in the Destroyer's shrine
The world is on the boil, bats in malodorous dark
Under a pyramid of writhing sculpture
That rams the destroying sky …
. . . .
The bats like microbes stitch heir hectic zigzag
Of black on black, of blind on blind, and dot
And carry and dot and carry and sizzle like seaweed
That reeks on the shore of the Infinite.[63]

The confident repetition, the rush of activity managed by lines that cross the line break and rhymes and half rhymes that wait a line or two for completion, often internal, sometimes jammed almost together, all capture the crash of the human against the infinite and the profusion of Hindu gods in this dazzling aural invocation of the shrine to Shiva.

MacNeice is dealing with a real place and real experiences, and that sense of the palpable gives 'Didymus' a strength many of his longer poems lack. In 'Didymus' the examples are specific, the invocations literal: 'Roses and sandalwood, | Red spittle on the flagstones of the temple, | Green flash of parrots, phosphorescent waves, | Caparisoned elephants and sacred bulls'.[64] Here is the full riot of life, and here, amidst all, 'to flout your banyan riot of dialectic', has come, in lines that suddenly slow, one 'With trouble in his eyes and tarry hands | And no sophistication and no caste', one 'armed with two crossed sticks' not a 'prince', nor a 'sage', nor a 'god', but 'Doubting Thomas'.[65] And here, beside the all-encompassing chaotic celebration of life and death, of chaos and creation, is the 'Church of the Little Mount', where

> says the plaque, here in Madras
> Before Madras or madeira was heard of
> Here was the hiding place of the saint
> Who had left his faith to his hands.[66]

MacNeice offers a portrait of a very human man, contrasted to 'Peter [who] would have talked big and John | [who would] Have called forth a serpent' and 'Paul [who] would have matched them abstract with abstract', men for whom 'even doubting, | For those dark and sly and chameleon minds | Was a technique they knew'.[67] But Thomas thinks of a man of whom he 'could no longer remember his face | Nor most of his words, he could only remember | That his nets were repaired on time', a very practical matter.[68]

And then comes Thomas's prayer, the third section of the poem, held together not just with internal rhymes and rhymes of the second and fourth lines of each quatrain, but buoyed, too, by the sustained use of homophones or, on occasion, homonyms (with one near miss) every first and third line of the seven quatrains that comprise the section. It is a prayer of doubt – the word appears nine times and the word 'redoubt' once – and of determination, terribly modern, a poem and a prayer not of faith but of hope to have faith again, and it is a prayer perfectly designed for radio, a linguistic and aural demonstration of all that radio and poetry together could be. Where on the page some of those homophones might look forced, the repetition clumsy, when heard they have quite another effect, connecting the words and ideas, transcending the language and offering an auditory evocation of a human tormented and determined:

> Whatever the clime, my task is ever to climb
>   Foothills that never are mountains; this Indian sky
> Is bowed with the dour monsoon and I doubt but soon
>   All of my converts and most of my work must die.
>
> I doubt that I have the least right to preach or write
>   In the name of Christ, I doubt that my doubt can find
> One hint that my terrible role could aspire to roll
>   The stone from the door of the tomb of the Indian mind.
>
> I doubt and I doubt; in a crumbling exposed redoubt,
>   Enfiladed by heathendom, here to the end
> I watch in the endless rain to herald the reign
>   Of the Friend of Man – but can he be Thomas's friend?[69]

MacNeice had seen the joy of faith on his father's face each Easter. He knew the uncertainty of doubt that must accompany those for whom 'foothills … are never mountains' and for whom life was a matter of making meaning despite the triviality, the futility of the gesture; but if there were indeed a meaning that transcends the temporal then 'each rice-farmer, snake-charmer, scavenger, merchant, mahout, | Each life in this land that is sore has the chance to soar'.[70] MacNeice's hope remained deeply inclusive, embracing all those who had reason to construct a life that was about more than the 'mere deliberating what to do'.[71] Yet in the end he was painfully aware, terrified even, that faith might fail him and that he would need to know, like Thomas, whose 'hands … once | Were tested and proved, yet failed through needing a test'.[72]

Yet ultimately, Thomas had chosen to make his knowledge the tool by which he might redeem not his faith but his faith in faith: 'If never there, | The Indies yet can show in a bare church | On a bare plaque the bare but adequate tribute | To one who had thrust his fingers into the wounds of God.'[73]

NOTES

References to the poems of Louis MacNeice are as they appear in Peter McDonald (ed.), *Collected Poems* (London: Faber, 2007), except as noted.

1   T.S. Eliot, 'The Metaphysical Poets', rev. of *Metaphysical Lyrics and Poems of the Seventeenth Century: Donne to Butler*, ed. Herbert J.C. Grierson (Oxford: Clarendon Press, 1921), *The Times Literary Supplement*, 1031 (20 October 1921), pp.669–70 (p.669).

2   T.S. Eliot, 'The Waste Land', *The Criterion*, 1 (October 1922), pp.50–64; *Four Quartets* (London: Faber, 1943).

3   Barry Unsworth, *Morality Play* (London: Hamish Hamilton, 1995), p.65.

4   Louis MacNeice, 'Epitaph for Liberal Poets', pp.231–2 (p.231).

5   George Herbert, 'Providence', *The Complete English Poems*, ed. John Tobin (London: Penguin, 2005), pp.108–113 (p.110).

6   George Herbert, 'Sighs and Groans', *The Complete English Poems*, p.76.

7   Louis MacNeice, 'Prayer before Birth', pp.213–14 (p.213).

8   Job 3: 3–6.

9   Job 3: 26.

10   Louis MacNeice, 'An Alphabet of Literary Prejudices', *Windmill*, 3:9 (March 1948), pp. 38–42; repr. in Alan Heuser (ed.), *Selected Literary Criticism of Louis MacNeice* (Oxford: Clarendon Press, 1987), pp.141–8 (p.148).

11   MacNeice, 'Prayer before Birth', p.213.

12   Ibid., p.214.

13   Louis MacNeice, 'Introductory Note' to 'The March Hare Resigns', in *The Dark Tower and Other Radio Scripts* (London: Faber, 1947), pp.136–7 (p.137).

14   Louis MacNeice, 'The Casualty (in memoriam G.H.S.)', pp.237–40 (p.237).

15   Ibid., p.238.

16   Ibid., pp.238–9.

17   Ibid., p.239.

18   Ibid., p.240.

19   Louis MacNeice, 'The News-reel', pp.240–1 (p.241).

20   Ibid.

21   Louis MacNeice, 'The Springboard', pp.235–6 (p.235).

22   Louis MacNeice, *Varieties of Parable* (Cambridge: Cambridge University Press, 1965), p.21.

23   MacNeice, 'The Springboard', p.235.

24   John Frederick MacNeice, 'Bishop's Christmas Message, 1935' in John Frederick MacNeice, *Our First Loyalty* (Belfast: Erskine Mayne, 1937), pp.80–2 (p.81).

25   Louis MacNeice, 'The Kingdom', pp.241–9 (I, p.242).

26   Ibid.

27   Ibid.

28   Ibid., II, p.242.

29   Canon Richard Clarke, a long-time friend and colleague of the bishop, delivered the funeral oration.

30   Louis MacNeice, 'The Kingdom', VII, pp.247–8.

31 Oakfield House bordered what is now the Woodland Trust's Oakfield Glen. The property included 'an enclosed cobbled courtyard complete with bell tower and beautiful terraced lawns rolling down to the sea. There was a very pretty little gingerbread gate lodge on the quarter-mile-long drive, also a couple of very large monkey puzzles, a Victorian ice house in the cliff face of the glen. It was rumoured there was a tunnel from St Nicholas's Church in Carrickfergus to the back of the ice house, but if there was we never found it' ('Spotlight: Oakfield Glen', *Broadleaf* [autumn 2014], unpaginated insert in issues distributed in Northern Ireland).

32 Barbara Coulton, *Louis MacNeice in the BBC* (London: Faber, 1980), p.78.

33 Louis MacNeice to Laurence Gilliam, 14 July 1945 (MS BBC), cited in *Letters of Louis MacNeice*, ed. Jonathan Allison (London: Faber, 2010), p.456.

34 Louis MacNeice, 'Notes', in *The Dark Tower and Other Radio Scripts* (London: Faber, 1947), pp.197–202 (p.202).

35 Matt. 5:14: 'Ye are the light of the world. A city that is set on a hill cannot be hid'.

36 John Boyd, 'Comment', *Lagan: A Miscellany of Ulster Writing*, 2:1[No. 4] (1946), [p.2].

37 Ibid., [p.1]

38 Louis MacNeice, *The Dark Tower*, in *The Dark Tower*, p.23.

39 Ibid., p.21.

40 Ibid., p.50.

41 Ibid., p.35. [Italics in the original.]

42 Ibid., p.55.

43 Louis MacNeice, *Autumn Sequel*, XXII, p.472.

44 Louis MacNeice, 'Letter to Graham and Anne Shepard', in W.H. Auden and Louis MacNeice, *Letters from Iceland* (London: Faber, 1937), pp.31–5 (p.33).

45 Peter Porter, 'The Achievement of Auden', *Sydney Studies in English*, 4 (1978) pp.73–113 (p.94).

46 It might perhaps be usefully noted that the 1944 English translation rendered the Danish *Begrebet Angest* as *Concept of Dread*. The current standard edition in English is Søren Kierkegaard, *Concept of Anxiety: A Simple Psychologically Orienting Deliberation on the Dogmatic Issue of Hereditary Sin*, ed. and trans. Reidar Thomte, Kierkegaard's Writings VIII (Princeton: Princeton University Press, 1981).

47 McDonald, William, 'Søren Kierkegaard', *The Stanford Encyclopedia of Philosophy* (winter 2014 edition), ed. Edward N. Zalta, <http://plato.stanford.edu/archives/win2014/entries/kierkegaard/>, accessed 19 February 2015.

48 Catherine Pickstock explores the idea of repetition and identity, relying on 'Snow' on more than one occasion, in *Repetition and Identity: The Literary Agenda* (Oxford: Oxford University Press, 2013).

49 Louis MacNeice, *Autumn Sequel*, XV, p.438.

50 Louis MacNeice, 'Hiatus', p.254.

51 Louis MacNeice, 'Carrick Revisited', pp.261–2 (p.262).

52 Louis MacNeice, 'The Strand', pp.263–4 (p.263).

53 Louis MacNeice, 'Woods', pp.271–2 (p.271).

54 Ibid., p.272.

55 Ibid.

56 Louis MacNeice, 'Corner Seat', p.255.

57 Louis MacNeice, 'Slow Movement', p.279–80, (p.280).

58 Louis MacNeice, 'The Stygian Banks,' pp.282–95, (III, p.286).

59 Psalm 66:13.

60 Louis MacNeice to Borden Stevenson, 31 March 1953; qtd in Robyn Marsack, *The Cave of Making: The Poetry of Louis MacNeice* (Oxford: Clarendon, 1982), p.96.

61 This reading of Brunetière is taken from Donald Davie, *A Gathered Church: The Literature of the English Dissenting Interest, 1700–1930* (New York: Oxford University Press, 1978), p.26. Brunetière was commenting on John Calvin's *Institutes* in a lecture given in Geneva on 17 December 1901.

62 Marsack, *The Cave of Making*, p.98, quoting Louis MacNeice to Terence Tiller, 21 April 1951.

63 Louis MacNeice, 'Didymus', pp.332–7 (I, p.332).

64 Ibid.

65 Ibid., p.333.

66 Ibid., II, p.333.

67 Ibid., p.334.

68 Ibid.

69 Ibid., III, p.335.

70 Ibid., pp.335–6.

71 Louis MacNeice, *Autumn Journal*, XIV, p.134.

72 MacNeice, 'Didymus', IV, p.337.

73 Ibid.

CHAPTER 9

The Last Test

The Britain to which the MacNeices returned from Greece was one in limbo. Tea, sugar, meat and some other foods were still rationed. The post-war Labour government had been replaced in October 1951 by a Conservative one led by the aging Winston Churchill. The country started to divest itself of colonies, unwilling in many cases to fight to keep them, aware of a lack of popular will at home to do so and of the military and economic strains in places where it did choose to oppose independence. At the same time, the idea of the Commonwealth was gaining popularity and the newly independent members were greeted with some affection in the public imagination, even as their citizens were often both needed and unwelcome in a Britain still mired in economic uncertainty.

MacNeice's work reflected the national condition: it both explored new ground and looked backward, unable, ultimately, to settle in one camp or the other. The MacNeices's choice of housing when they returned captured this state of betweenness. Elizabeth Bowen had decided to return to Éire for good – she would commit the rest of her life to trying to preserve Bowen Court and to writing its history – and Louis asked T.S. Eliot whether he and Hedli might be able to acquire the lease of the property Bowen was surrendering. This was not necessarily a simple transaction, for Bowen was moving out of 2 Clarence Terrace, a Regency period home overlooking Regent's Park. It was owned by the Crown Estate and beside an ability to pay the rent the estate then expected its tenants to be of suitable moral stature, and MacNeice's status as a re-married divorcé could conceivably have been a complicating factor. Nonetheless, in July 1952, the house went from being the London home of an Irish writer who recognised the importance of change but retained a fondness for an earlier time and place, to being that of an Irish writer who recognised the importance of change but retained a longing for an earlier time and place he had never quite known.

At about the same time, MacNeice signed a contract with Dan Davin at Oxford University Press to edit, with W.R. Rodgers, a collection of essays on the 'Character of Ireland.' He was to write a verse introduction, Rodgers a verse conclusion. They recruited contributors – Bowen, John Hewitt, Sam Hanna Bell and Denis Johnston among them – but the collection never made it to fruition, in part because of the copious amount of drinking its editors engaged in, both separately and when together. All in all, the project was either 'a failure in collaboration or a collaboration in failure'.[1] But there remained also the problem that the character of Ireland is a concept easy to grasp in cliché but hard to discuss with cohesive subtlety.

One creative outlet MacNeice pursued was adapting for radio what was perhaps his favourite poem, Edmund Spenser's *The Faerie Queene*. His twelve-part adaptation was broadcast on the Third Programme in the last three months of 1952, preceded by his own introductory explanation of the poem's enduring power. It was a poem he'd been considering in a different context at least since 1944, when he had told Eliot that *Springboard* would mark an end as well as a beginning. He was thinking, he said, of writing a long poem in some manner 'comparable to the "Faerie Queene" in its interlocking episodes, sub-plots, and digressions which aren't really digressions'.[2] Quite how much he had Spenser's poem in mind as he worked on what would become *Autumn Sequel* is not at all clear, but critics certainly identified digressions aplenty, where, that is, they found any sort of guiding narrative from which to digress. One review noted that 'in calling his new long poem in twenty-six cantos of that very intractable metre in English, terza rima, "a rhetorical poem" Mr MacNeice rather cunningly anticipates the verdict of the reader, that the poem is a triumph not only of skill but of determination'.[3] Even so,

> passages expressing personal feeling … are deeply moving; so also are passages of moral exhortation, on the importance of being and making, of struggling and giving and loving, of not yielding to drift.

The whole poem is immensely readable, but it is in these personal and moral passages that we get farthest away from the sense of an exercise, of something extremely skilful but also perhaps too consciously and wilfully 'contrived'.[4]

As most critics noted, the biggest failure of *Autumn Sequel* is that it looks back on a life without getting past retrospection so the lack of a cohesive whole ultimately leaves most readers noticing the terza rima rather than the poem's content. MacNeice's powerful tribute to Dylan Thomas in the course of the poem reveals his own awareness of the challenge:

> we need not wait
> To meet his like; his like is seldom born,
> Being admitted through the Ivory Gate
>
> Where most must enter through the Gates of Horn.[5]

The strains of travel and their very different creative personalities were also beginning to test his relationship with Hedli. He took to spending long hours at the pub, 'standing in pubs' being among the activities he 'liked', even as he acknowledged that activity as one of his wife's 'dislikes'.[6] Hedli was an entertainer. The problem was not so much that Louis was not one for entertaining but that he was not much for being entertained. Their life had become itinerant, Clarence Terrace being a way station rather than a home, and neither of them quite knew how to navigate the waters in which they found themselves. MacNeice concluded Canto XIV of *Autumn Sequel* with the question 'Has he, or not, been here before?', recounting a dream of miners, 'in helmets, masks and mudstained overalls' passing him by deep underground in a procession reminiscent of his reworking in *Autumn Journal* of Charles Sorley's faceless soldiers.[7] And he surely knew the answer to be 'yes'.

His response was to concentrate on 'what in time the timeless vagrant finds',[8] as he phrased the theme in his introductory poem to the 1957 collection *Visitations*. Whither Britain might go five years into the reign of Elizabeth II or Éire with Eámon De Valera once again Taoiseach no longer seemed an issue. The Suez crisis of 1956 and the re-introduction of use of Part II of the Offences against the State Act in Éire in 1957 indicated how little had changed in the years since the war.

The title, *Visitations*, recalled MacNeice's exploration of the consequences and comforts learned by Odysseus and by Jacob in 'Day of Returning' in *Ten Burnt Offerings*, the lessons of men 'no more a vagrant | No more – except in flashes – a visionary, | No more a chooser'.[9] If not a vagrant, he was more a traveller than ever, and in the autumn of 1957 he was back in India, the frustrations of domestic life evident in a letter to Hedli that began, 'Where the hell are you? In Switzerland? I haven't heard a word.'[10] In Kuala Lumpur in November he was defending *Autumn Sequel* to her, 'a work which you, like Margaret G[ardiner], tend to crab'.[11] Perhaps it was not surprising he opened *Visitations* with an address 'To the Public'. It is a garrulous assertion of poetic licence: 'Why hold that poets are so sensitive? | A thickskinned grasping lot who filch and eavesdrop | Who enjoy themselves at other men's expense.'[12] But in a second address that followed those opening remarks he offered a perfectly crafted and heartfelt justification that anticipated not only the already apparent rise of television but also the growth of a broader universe of electronic media:

When books have all seized up like the books in graveyards
And reading and even speaking have been replaced
By other, less difficult media, we wonder if you
Will find in flowers and fruit the same colour and taste
They held for us for whom they were framed in words,
And will your grass be green, your sky be blue,
Or will your birds be always wingless birds?[13]

Ulster, Connemara and the rest of Éire were now 'A Hand of Snapshots'. MacNeice was a BBC producer with an office in London travelling where either script or fancy supported by a programming idea took him, but in his homeland he found

his thoughts return to the city as he fingers
His city tie, thinking he has made good,
Gone up in the world, on the whole, were it not for something,
Intuited perhaps though never understood,
Which flitted through this room around his cradle.

So, on his last day, walking beside his brother,
Whose dog like a black thought streaks through ditch and fence

Rounding up sheep, he sees in his brother a sudden something:
An oaf, but an oaf with dignity and the sense
That it is a fine day if it only rains a little.[14]

In Donegal, he had 'entered solitude once more to find communion | With other solitary beings, with the whole race of men'.[15] MacNeice's yearning for 'communion' outside of church foreshadows, perhaps, the appeal of a fellow son of a Church of Ireland mother whose loss hit him hard, Paul David Hewson: 'And I'd join the movement | If there was one I could believe in. | Yeah, I'd break bread and wine | If there was a church I could receive in'.[16]

In Sudan and Egypt in 1955 MacNeice had realised 'my passport lied | Calling me dark who am grey',[17] and in an almost Yeatsian act of re-creation responded by turning his individual life into a parable:

For his long-lost dragon lurked ahead,
Not to be dodged and never napping,
And he knew in his bones he was all but dead,
Yet that death was half the story.[18]

Sylvie, it turned out, had been waiting all along:

She stood where the water bubbled bright
On the near bank, the known bank;
He took her hand and they struck a light
And crossed the bridge and burnt it.
          . . . .
So, far they came and found no shore,
The waves falling, the night falling,
To board a ship sunk years before,
And all the world was daylight.[19]

His was now a life where grace came unexpectedly and offered only inklings of a distant world, yet

When the stranger came out of the night
Asking for bread and water
And, according to our lights and the moon's light,

We laid the table on the terrace,
Suddenly all of us felt a waft of danger,
Oddly blended with comfort from that stranger.

Though he spoke quite ordinary words,
Words of whence and whither,
And, according to our view or even a bird's
Eye view, was nobody special,
We felt a shiver in the scalp which seemed like fear –
And yet we wanted him to linger here.

So when he slipped off into the night
Thanking us for his supper
And then, by the moon's light and his own light,
Added that he was an angel,
We were a little, but not so much surprised;
For we had known him always, we realized.[20]

Where for his father grace had been a permanent promise, for the son those intimations of grace in the woman by the river or the angel who came for dinner left the question of how one might respond to their usual absence. It was a question MacNeice pursued on his return from a BBC training course for television in 1958. *One for the Grave* was never quite finished, but after MacNeice's death Frank Dermody used the last draft to open the new Abbey Theatre space as part of the 1966 Dublin Theatre Festival. It was, perhaps, a 'strange choice',[21] but Dermody was attracted to MacNeice's staging notes urging that 'the more the production can suggest the bustle of a real TV studio with its crowds of personnel and clutter of machines ... the better'.[22] Dermody took advantage of the new stage, and the large cast included Sinead Cusack, Stephen Rea and Geraldine Plunkett. Vincent Dowling played the role of the director and Pat Layde that of Everyman. The choice of *One for the Grave* recognised MacNeice's allure in the south, but the play itself is not noticeably Irish, although Joseph Ronsley has suggested it shares a 'close affinity' with Denis Johnston's *A Bride for the Unicorn*, originally staged on 9 May 1933 at the Gate Theatre.[23]

Everyman, 'middling well dressed and [who] might come from any sphere of society',[24] is very much the Everyman of the medieval morality plays. He is about to die, entering a TV studio unaware that he is embarking upon, as the floor manager puts it, 'a very peculiar sort of show because it's not a finished product – and never will be. In fact it's really a rehearsal but it's not a typical rehearsal because … well, there's only one of it. It's a sort of do-it-yourself job'.[25] Confronted with a review of his life – based on 'This is Your Life', the popular BBC television show hosted by Dublin native Eamonn Andrews – Everyman meets Conscience, who tells him 'You, when young, | Knew me a little – not for long – | And then you met this fellow here',[26] Lucre, who reminds him of 'Madrid in' '36' and of 'other countries, other spheres – | The League of Nations, the T.U.C., | In art or sport or God knows what | Selling the pass, selling the lot'.[27] The Irishman in MacNeice perhaps still resented the British and their allies for enabling the failure of the League; the reformer in him railed against those who had used the TUC (Trades Union Congress) for their own ends and he worried at the state of culture and of sports.[28]

There is no character in *One for the Grave* comparable to Sylvie in *The Dark Tower* to offer an alternative perspective, but where Roland's speech defending his life comes right at the end of the play and after his options have been exhausted, Everyman's defence comes halfway through Act II, when he turns to 'my fellows who *don't* know all the answers', telling the audience:

> I did not choose to put in this ring to fight, I did not ask to be born, but a babe in arms is in arms in more senses than one and since my birth I've been fighting. Conscript or volunteer – I just don't know which I am – and it may have been a losing battle but at least I've been in it, I've been in it. And *les jeux sont faits* and *ne rien va plus*. To be a human being is a cause for grief – and for pride. Everyman must vindicate himself. Oh I know they say one has no choice in the matter, but I don't believe them. Do you?[29]

Seizing the initiative, Everyman announces that 'If I cannot conduct my life, at least I'll conduct my death'.[30] And while that death doesn't go as he had hoped, he is joined at the end by Conscience and Free Will, who accompany him to the grave, where the gravedigger, who sounds like Everyman's father, only 'kinder',[31] leads him through a final prayer to 'Thou whoever Thou art', which ends with Everyman acknowledging he has 'sinned against life and myself' but thankful for 'the chance' and asking that 'If I failed to use it, forgive me', a conclusion that recalls the invocation of the 'Prayer Before Birth'. And, indeed, the gravedigger points out that 'Most people think I'm the end but I am also the beginning. I was present when your mother bore you.'[32]

Family and Ireland remained intertwined and in 1956, the same year his stepmother died, MacNeice had written and produced *Carpe Diem* for the Third Programme, a tribute to the Roman poet, Horace. It, too, smacks of reflection rather than anticipation, but it offers one last glimpse of his father, confusing his politics but placing him outside both Éire's and Northern Ireland's later political developments: 'My father – he'd supported Asquith over Home Rule but he strongly disapproved of the Easter Rising.'[33] Six months before *Carpe Diem* aired, Bea Greer died on 8 April and MacNeice returned once more to Carrickfergus, where her coffin was placed in his father's old church in preparation for her funeral. By then, his father had been immortalised on an exterior wall of St Nicholas in a corbel cast while he was Bishop of Cashel, and his pastoral staff, carved from bog oak by Thomas McGregor Greer, Bea's brother, rested on display in the church sanctuary. Elizabeth returned, too, and Willie made the journey from nearby Oakfield House where he had lived with his stepmother since his father's death.[34] It was the last time all three MacNeice siblings were together in Ireland. Louis memorialised his stepmother in a tribute that conflated her funeral with a young boy's glimpse of the 'Titanic' 'forty long years ago',[35] but her death, the passing of the last close link to a culture of which he had always been wary but for which he nonetheless held affection, left him unsure whether to claim victory or admit defeat, illustrated by his confused account of his father's political instincts and his uncertainty when walking with his brother and his dog across fields they had known since childhood.

MacNeice continued to travel to Éire, and he was in Dublin for the 1957 England – Ireland match at Lansdowne Road, a game that might have inspired the comment in *One for the Grave* about the 'selling' of sport. England won 6–0 despite being a man down for much of the contest. MacNeice found the game 'savage and very disappointing, the most notable thing about it being that the crowd booed the referee – which I understand is unprecedented'.[36] Northern Ireland, too, still claimed him and in July 1957 he received an honorary DLitt from Queen's University, Belfast, six months before being named a CBE (Commander of the Order of the British Empire) in the New Year's Honours list. That the academic recognition came from Belfast rather than Dublin underscores fault lines

MacNeice did not always manage to avoid. Queen's was comfortable acknowledging the son of a Church of Ireland bishop with a senior position in the BBC. Trinity College, Dublin, had honoured the father with a DPhil in 1931, as was then customary for newly appointed bishops in the Church of Ireland, but it had not been impressed by the son's attempt in 1939 to secure the chair of English. By 1957, it was clear that however many rugby matches MacNeice attended, and however many bars he drank in, he remained an outsider even in Dublin's Anglophile cultural circles.

Complicating matters, MacNeice was one of the perceived leaders of the 'Third Programme Irish'.[37] Not everyone in Éire appreciated what was assumed to be the cultural (and economic) dominance of a coterie including MacNeice, Rodgers and Johnston. That they regularly provided work for people such as Dominic Behan, younger brother of Brendan, and Seán Ó Faoláin did not protect them from jibes such as that delivered by the older Behan:

> my brother … is married to a Glasgow girl … [who] only gets angry with me when I take the mickey out of him and other third programme Irish Keeners … God knows, if ever the English (radio licence holders anyway) had an excuse for a pogrom against the Irish, they have it in the BBC.[38]

Patrick Kavanagh was even more scathing about the cultural effects of the BBC, castigating Rodgers's long-running series 'Irish Literary Portraits':[39]

> How did you bury Joyce?
> In a broadcast symposium.
> That's how we buried Joyce
> To a tuneful encomium.
>
> Who carried the coffin out?
> Six Dublin Codgers
> Led into Langham Place
> By W.R. Rodgers.[40]

Yet MacNeice would produce Kavanagh's *The Great Hunger* for the BBC, and he had been sympathetic, at least, to the attempt to foster regional literature in the shape of such publications as *Lagan*, which was inspired in part by Geoffrey Taylor's *The Bell*, which, John Hewitt said, provided evidence that for Ulster writers 'Dublin was our literary capital'.[41] He also retained a keen awareness of current Irish authors, praising Samuel Beckett's lyricism on several occasions, and in South Africa in autumn 1959 he gave a series of lectures that included one on 'The Irish Playwrights'.[42] Taylor, incidentally, thought *Autumn Sequel* to be MacNeice's 'high water mark', even going so far as to say 'there has been no higher in a hundred years'.[43]

In the midst of travel and a failing marriage – Hedli finally told him to leave in September 1960[44] – an increasing sense of dislocation struck him. The final few poems of what would be his penultimate collection, *Solstices*, underscore that mood. He revisited familiar tropes, but not places, from his earlier works. He continued to wonder at the hints of a near yet reachable life: 'The mirror above my fireplace reflects the reflected | Room in my window'.[45] The reflections in those reflections ultimately find him where

> my indoors rooms lie stranded,
> Where a taxi perhaps will drive in through the bookcase
> Whose books are not for reading and past the fire
> Which gives no warmth and pull up by my desk
> At which I cannot write since I am not lefthanded.[46]

Being between things was still a constant refrain, and he reflected on professional and personal hopes he had once had, offering a stark identification of both his own and Ireland's troubles with memory: 'A house can be haunted by those who were never there | If there was where they were missed', and 'A life can be haunted by what it never was | If that were merely glimpsed'.[47]

Time was running out, 'Lost in the maze | That means yourself and never out of the wood | These days, though lost, will be all your days'.[48] But for all his classics training that shows up in poems such as 'Variations on Heraclitus' MacNeice was unable to find a path out of the woods.[49] Highlighting this pattern, *Solstices* concludes with a 24-line single-sentence poem written for a woman he had met in South Africa and who was not the first he had become almost instantly infatuated with. Apparently without irony it was called 'All Over Again'.[50]

No longer in a marriage, out of his house, infatuated again back in England, this time with Mary Wimbush, the actress widely known for various BBC roles, MacNeice also found himself back in the business of working relentlessly to pay the bills. He had taken a part-time position in 1961 with the BBC as it underwent one of its periodic retrenchments. That allowed him to sign a contract for what would become his bestselling book, *Astrology*, a work the flap copy describes as a 'unique book [by] Louis MacNeice – poet, playwright, and scholar – [who] takes an astringent, unprejudiced look at astrology in all its aspects',[51] by which the publishers might as well have meant that the book is an omnivorous gathering of easily found material with no apparent critical judgment applied to its selection.

In the midst of dislocation, one constant remained – his interest in Irish rugby – but now the internationals were not so much a match added onto existing work-related travel as a financial opportunity in their own right. In early 1961 he pitched the editor of the *New Statesman* a story on the Ireland – England match in Dublin, a proposal sweetened by the suggestion the article be about the game only in so far as it served as a microcosm of the 'Brains and Brawns of Dublin'.[52] He planned on staying with 'a large farmer who once played in the second row for Ireland in a disastrous match against the South Africans'.[53] This would be MacNeice's introduction to the 'Brawns. As for the Brains, they are lying about in all directions'.[54] He mentioned Honor Tracy, Ó Faoláin, Austin Clarke, Kavanagh and Brendan Behan among others. And whatever his reservations about the BBC, he was proud enough of Radio Éireann to tell his correspondent it had 'just become a corporation like the BBC instead of being a branch of the post office',[55] headed by Andrews, upon whose most famous show MacNeice had modeled *One for the Grave*. John Freeman offered MacNeice 20 guineas for the story, but although he attended the match no article appeared, MacNeice never quite getting past the pre- and post-game consummation of whiskey and Guinness, although he blamed the failure on his driver running out of petrol.[56]

MacNeice also tried to sell Faber on the idea of a selection of his poems specifically connected to place, the best justification for which that he could muster was that many of them had appeared in neither his earlier collected edition nor in *Eighty-Five Poems*. Faber rejected the idea as potentially insulting to readers who might have preferred new poems. In the same letter, MacNeice added, 'by the way, I hope to knock off that children's story soon',[57] a reference to an idea he had suggested to Faber after it had published his children's book, *The Sixpence that Rolled Away* in 1956. Nothing came of that, but the sense of urgency in MacNeice's financial position is well indicated by that phrase 'knock off'.

1963 came and MacNeice had an agreement with the BBC to produce his drama *Persons from Porlock*, the title paying tribute to Samuel Taylor Coleridge but with 'Death' as the Porlockian. He would also complete a volume for Faber that opens with a stunningly evocative and controlled poem, 'Soap Suds', remembering Seapark, where his stepmother had lived until her marriage into the MacNeice family. The scent of soap familiar from long before triggers a memory that begins with croquet on a perfectly manicured lawn. The ball progresses through the hoops that are the hoops of the game and also of life, until the recognition comes that 'the ball is lost and the mallet slipped long since from the hands | Under the running tap that are not the hands of a child'.[58]

He addressed a poem to Horace, whom he had admired for so long, telling the older poet of the 'Old lag's tip in the lobby: "Plead guilty | Before they acquit you and adopt you"', and suggesting that 'To opt out now seems better than capitulate | To the too well-lighted and over-advertised | Idols of the age'.[59] And he concluded the volume with 'Coda':

Maybe we knew each other better
When the night was young and unrepeated
And the moon stood still over Jericho.[60]

So much for the past; in the present
There are moments caught between heart-beats
When maybe we know each other better.

But what is that clinking in the darkness?
Maybe we shall know each other better
When the tunnels meet beneath the mountain.[61]

In August, MacNeice went to Yorkshire with a recording engineer to get exactly right the sounds from beneath the mountain he needed for *Persons from Porlock*. It is easy to see the hand of fate in the viral pneumonia he apparently contracted while wet, cold and tired throughout the expedition. He refused at first to go to hospital but his sister, the doctor, the care-giver of their brother, the one remaining link to Carrickfergus and the Mac Niss games, made it clear that hospital was where he should be. So he went. And did not get better. And it is hard not to wonder at his choice of a title for his final volume – *The Burning Perch* – with its careful inclusion of a definite article and its author's ambivalence about its title, which he finally settled on when revising the printer's proofs.

NOTES

References to the poems of Louis MacNeice are as they appear in Peter McDonald (ed.), *Collected Poems* (London: Faber, 2007), except as noted.

1 Peter McDonald, 'The Fate of "Identity": John Hewitt, W. R. Rodgers and Louis MacNeice', *The Irish Review*, 12 (spring-summer, 1992), pp.72–86 (p.83).
2 Louis MacNeice to T.S. Eliot, 7 April 1944, pp.449–50.
3 G.S. Fraser, 'The Poetry of Consciousness', rev. of *Autumn Sequel: A Rhetorical Poem in XXVI Cantos* by Louis MacNeice (London: Faber, 1954), *Times Literary Supplement*, 2756 (26 November 1954), p.754.
4 Ibid.
5 Louis MacNeice, *Autumn Sequel*, XVIII, p.452. See, the *Odyssey*, 19, pp.560–9. Penelope, who has had a dream that Odysseus is about to return, suspects the dream is false: 'For two are the gates of shadowy dreams, and one is fashioned of horn and one of ivory. Those dreams that pass through the gate of sawn ivory deceive men ... But those that come forth through the gate of polished horn bring true issues to pass, when any mortal sees them.' [Homer, *The Odyssey*, trans. Arthur T. Murray, rev. George E. Dimock (Cambridge, MA: Harvard University Press, 1995), Vol. 2.]
6 Qtd in Jon Stallworthy, *Louis MacNeice* (London: Faber, 1995), p.407.
7 MacNeice, *Autumn Sequel*, XIV, p.437.
8 Louis MacNeice, 'To Hedli', p.494.
9 Louis MacNeice, 'Day of Returning', pp.355–9 (p.359).
10 Louis MacNeice to Hedli Anderson, 23 October [1957], p.620. Her parents lived in Switzerland.
11 Same to same, 9 November [1957], p.628.
12 Louis MacNeice, 'To the Public', p.495.
13 Louis MacNeice, 'To Posterity', p.495.
14 Louis MacNeice, 'A Hand of Snapshots', 'THE BACK-AGAIN', pp.501–2 (p.502).
15 Louis MacNeice, 'Donegal Triptych', III, pp.500–1 (p.501).
16 U2 (music) and Bono (words), 'Acrobat', *Achtung Baby* [track 11], prod. Daniel Lanois, Island Records, 1991.
17 Louis MacNeice, 'Beni Hasan', p.506.
18 Louis MacNeice, 'The Burnt Bridge', pp.513–15 (p.514).
19 Ibid., p.515.
20 Louis MacNeice, 'Visitations', V, pp.521–2.
21 Robert Welch, *The Abbey Theatre, 1899–1999: Form and Pressure* (Oxford: Oxford University Press, 1999), p.181.

22 Louis MacNeice, 'Notes', in *One for the Grave: A Modern Morality Play* (London: Faber, 1968), pp.13–14 (p.14).

23 Joseph Ronsely (ed.), *Denis Johnston, a Retrospective*. Irish Literary Studies 8 (Gerrards Cross: Colin Smythe, 1981), p.166.

24 MacNeice, *One for the Grave*, p.20.

25 Ibid., p.20.[Ellipsis in the original.]

26 Ibid., p.28.

27 Ibid., p.29.

28 Ibid., pp.32–3.

29 Ibid., p.74. [Italics in the original.] *Les jeux sont faits* is a reference to the Jean-Paul Sartre play known in English as 'The Chips Are Down'.

30 Ibid., p.75.

31 Ibid., p.85.

32 Ibid., p.86.

33 Louis MacNeice, *Carpe Diem*, dir. Louis MacNeice, BBC Third Programme, 8 October 1956; printed in *Louis MacNeice: The Classical Radio Plays*, ed. Amanda Wrigley and S. J. Harrison (Oxford: Oxford University Press, 2013), pp.365–92 (p.387).

34 Alicia St Leger, 'Louis MacNeice: Poet, Writer and Broadcaster 1907–1963', exhibition and community outreach programme to accompany the exhibition at Carrickfergus Museum, September to December 2007 (Carrickfergus: Carrickfergus Borough Council, 2007), p.14.

35 Louis MacNeice, 'Death of an Old Lady', p.517.

36 Louis MacNeice to Denis Johnston, 5 March 1957, p.615.

37 The term 'third programme Irish' seems to have been coined by Brendan Behan.

38 Brendan Behan to the *New Statesman*, ? December 1962 [unpublished], in Brendan Behan and E.H. Mikhail (eds), *The Letters of Brendan Behan* (London: Macmillan, 1992), p.216.

39 A selection of these were published as, W.R. Rodgers, *Irish Literary Portraits* (London: BBC, 1972). Rodgers would often interview various people for each episode and then splice the interviews together to create the illusion they were speaking to each other, creating a fine case study for a media ethics class.

40 Patrick Kavanagh, 'Who Killed James Joyce?' *Envoy*, 5:17 (1951), p.62; cited in Claire Wills, *The Best Are Leaving: Emigration and Post-War Irish Culture* (Cambridge: Cambridge University Press, 2015). Langham Place is the location of Broadcasting House.

41 Qtd in Edna Longley, 'The Whereabouts of Literature', in Gerard Carruthers, David Goldie and Alastair Renfrew (eds), *Beyond Scotland: New Contexts for Twentieth-Century Scottish Literature* (Amsterdam: Rodopi, 2004), pp.151–66 (p.159).

42 Stallworthy, *MacNeice*, p.438.

43 Geoffrey Taylor to Louis MacNeice, 15 November 1954, p.628n.

44 Stallworthy, *MacNeice*, p.438.

45 Louis MacNeice, 'Reflections', p.561.

46 Ibid.

47 Louis MacNeice, 'Selva Oscura', pp.571–2 (p.571, p.572).

48 Ibid., p.572.

49 Louis MacNeice, 'Variations on Heraclitus', p.560.

50 Louis MacNeice, 'All Over Again', pp.572–3.

51   Louis MacNeice, *Astrology* (London: Aldus, 1964), flap copy.

52   Louis MacNeice to John Freeman, 27 January 1961, p.673.

53   South Africa won 17–5 at Lansdowne Road on 8 December 1951. The two Irish locks were Robin Thompson and Patrick Lawlor. Thompson became a media commentator after playing rugby league in England. He captained the Lions but never Ireland nor Ulster. He would seem to be the obvious candidate for the person MacNeice was staying with, except that he was a Queen's chemistry graduate and his brains were at least on a par with his brawn. However, it seems most unlikely MacNeice would have known Lawlor or that Lawlor was a farmer. He was born in Marino on Dublin's north side and played for Clontarf. He was, incidentally, the last surviving of the 'Ravenhill Rebels' and thus played a small part in bringing MacNeice to Dublin so often. On 27 February 1954 the 'rebels' refused to take the field for the British national anthem if it were played for the Irish team. A compromise saved the game (Ireland 6–0 Scotland) but Ireland would not play rugby again at Ravenhill until the 24 August 2007 World Cup warm-up match against Italy (Ireland 23–20 Italy). The best account of the events leading to that day in 1954 is at <http://www.theguardian.com/sport/2007/feb/27/comment.gdnsport3>.

54   MacNeice to Freeman, 27 January 1961, p.673.

55   Ibid. Radio Éireann became a corporation on 1 June 1960.

56   Jonathan Allison, ed., *Letters of Louis MacNeice*, p.673n.

57   Louis MacNeice to Charles Monteith, 15 September 1961, pp.681–2.

58   Louis MacNeice, 'Soap Suds', p.577.

59   Louis MacNeice 'Memoranda to Horace', pp.603–7 (V, p.607).

60   A reference to Joshua 10:13, 'And the sun stood still, and the moon stayed, until the people had avenged themselves upon their enemies', but perhaps also to the district of Oxford where the Beazleys had lived and where he had met his first wife.

61   Louis MacNeice, 'Coda', p.610.

Works Cited

Adams, Bernard, *Denis Johnston: A Life* (Dublin: Lilliput, 2002).

Aitken, Ian, 'Coal Face', BFI Screen Online, <http://www.screenonline.org.uk/film/id/461606/>.

Allison, Jonathan(ed.), *Letters of Louis MacNeice* (London: Faber, 2010).

Andrews, Kevin, 'Time and the Will Lie Sidestepped: Athens, the Interval', in Terence Brown and Alec Reid (eds), *Time Was Away* (Dublin: Dolmen, 1974), pp.103–10.

Armitage, C[hristopher] M[ead] and Neil Clark, *A Bibliography of the Works of Louis MacNeice* (Edmonton: University of Alberta Press, 1973).

Assisi, St Francis of, *Laudes creaturarum* ['Canticle of the Sun'], <http://drc.usask.ca/projects/faulkner/main/related_texts/st_francis_canticle.html#1>.

Auden, W[ystan] H[ugh], *Another Time: Poems* (New York, NY: Random House, 1940).

——— *The Age of Anxiety: A Baroque Eclogue* (New York, NY: Random House, 1947).

——— and Louis MacNeice, *Letters from Iceland* (London: Faber, 1937).

Aurelius, Marcus, *The Thoughts of the Emperor Marcus Aurelius Antoninus*, trans. George Long (Boston: 1894).

Banks-Smith, Nancy, 'The Dismal Diary of Adrienne Mole', *The Guardian*, 4 February 1994, in Alan Rusbridger (ed.), *The Guardian Year '94*, (London: Fourth Estate, 1994), pp.237–40.

Behan, Brendan and E[dward] H[alim] Mikhail (eds), *The Letters of Brendan Behan* (London: Macmillan, 1992).

Bell, Kathleen, 'Nancy Spender's Recollections of Wystan Auden', *W.H. Auden Society Newsletter*, 10 and 11 (September 1993), pp.1–3.

Berry, Sterling, 'The Ethics of War: A Reply', *Irish Church Quarterly*, 8:30 (April 1915), pp.102–11.

Berryman, John, *The Dream Songs* (New York, NY: Farrar, Strauss and Giroux, 1969).

Blake, William, *Milton: A Poem* (London: 1804).

Bowen, Elizabeth, 'Notes on Éire', *Espionage Reports to Winston Churchill, 1940–2: With a Review of Irish Neutrality in World War II*, ed. Jack Lane and Brendan Clifford (Millstreet: Aubane Historical Society, 1999).

Boyd, John, 'Comment', *Lagan: A Miscellany of Ulster Writing*, 2:1 [No.4] (1946), np.

Braund, Susanna Morton (ed. and trans.), *Juvenal and Persius*, Loeb Classical Library 91 (Cambridge, MA: Harvard University Press, 2004).

Britten, Benjamin, *Letters from a Life: The Selected Letters and Diaries of Benjamin Britten 1913–1976* Vol 2, *1939–45*, ed. Donald Mitchell and Philip Reed (London: Faber, 1991).

Brown, John (ed.), *In the Chair: Interviews with Poets from the North of Ireland* (Cliffs of Moher: Salmon, 2002).

Brown, Richard Danson, 'Neutrality and Commitment: MacNeice, Yeats, Ireland and the Second World War', *Journal of Modern Literature*, 28:3 (spring 2005), pp.109–29.

Brown, Terence, 'Louis MacNeice and the "Dark Conceit"', *Ariel*, 3:4 (October 1972), pp.16–24.

Campbell, Roy, *Talking Bronco* (London: Faber, 1946).

Candlish, Stewart and Pierfrancesco Basile, 'Francis Herbert Bradley', *The Stanford Encyclopedia of Philosophy* (spring 2013), ed. Edward N. Zalta, <http://plato.stanford.edu/archives/spr2013/entries/bradley/>.

Carpenter, Humphrey, *W. H. Auden: A Biography* (Boston, MA: Houghton Mifflin, 1981).

Carson, Ciaran, *Belfast Confetti* (Oldcastle: Gallery, 1989).

Clarke, John, *The Even More Complete Book of Australian Verse* (Melbourne: Text, 2003).

Coulton, Barbara, *Louis MacNeice in the BBC* (London: Faber, 1980).

Cronin, Gloria L. and Ben Siegel (eds), *Conversations with Robert Penn Warren* (Jackson, MS: University Press of Mississippi, 2005).

Cronin, Sean, *Frank Ryan – The Search for The Republic* (Dublin: Repsol, 1980).

Crowe, Catriona, Ronan Fanning, Michael Kennedy, Eunan O'Halpin and Dermot Keogh (eds), *Documents on Irish Foreign Policy* Vol. VI, *1939–1941* (Dublin: Royal Irish Academy, 2008).

Davie, Donald, *A Gathered Church: The Literature of the English Dissenting Interest, 1700–1930* (New York, NY: Oxford University Press, 1978).

Dodds, E[ric] R[obertson], 'Louis MacNeice at Birmingham', in Terence Brown and Alec Reid (eds), *Time Was Away: The World of Louis MacNeice* (Dublin: Dolmen, 1974), pp.35–38.

Dunn, Douglas, *Dante's Drum-Kit* (London: Faber, 1993).

Earp, F[rank] R[ussell], 'The *Agamemnon* and the *Bacchae* in English Verse', rev. of *The Agamemnon of Aeschylus*, trans. Louis MacNeice (London: Faber, 1936) and of *The Bacchae of Euripides*, trans. Francis Evelyn (London: Heath Cranton, 1936), *The Classical Review*, 51:4 (September 1937), pp.119–120.

'Éire: Against Everybody?' *Time*, 35:24 (10 June 1940), p.38.

Eliot, T[homas] S[tearns], *Prufrock and Other Observations* (London: The Egoist, 1917).

——— 'The Metaphysical Poets', rev. of *Metaphysical Lyrics and Poems of the Seventeenth Century: Donne to Butler*, ed. Herbert J[ohn] C[lifford] Grierson (Oxford: Clarendon, 1921), *Times Literary Supplement*, 1031 (20 October 1921), pp.669–70.

——— 'The Waste Land', *The Criterion*, 1 (October 1922), pp.50–64.

——— 'Introduction', in *Johnson's 'London' and 'The Vanity of Human Wishes'* (London: Haslewood, 1930), pp.9–17; repr. in Phyllis M[aud] Jones (ed.), *English Critical Essays: Twentieth Century* (London: Oxford University Press, 1947), pp.301–10.

——— *Four Quartets* (London: Faber, 1943).

Elman, Richard, 'The Legacy of Louis MacNeice', *The New Republic,* 149:17 (26 October 1963), p.19.

Engle, John, 'A Modest Refusal: Yeats, MacNeice, and Irish Poetry', in Deborah Fleming (ed.), *Learning the Trade: Essays on W.B. Yeats and Contemporary Poetry* (West Cornwall: Locust Hill, 1993), pp.71–88.

Ervine, St John Greer, *Sir Edward Carson and the Ulster Movement* (Dublin: Maunsel 1915).

——— *The Lady of Belmont: A Play in Five Acts* (London: Allen & Unwin, 1923).

Fallon, Brian, 'F. R. Higgins: A Neglected Master Craftsman', *The Irish Times*, 8 January 1991, p.8.

Firth, Katherine, '"Queen of the Boys Tonight": Hedli Anderson and the "Auden Gang"', Louis MacNeice Centenary Conference and Celebration, Queen's University, Belfast, September 2007, <https://www.academia.edu/3984288/Queen_of_the_boys_tonight_Hedli_Anderson_and_the_Auden_Gang_Katherine_Firth>.

Fitzgerald, Penelope, *Human Voices* (London: Flamingo, 1988).

FitzGibbon, Constantine, *The Blitz* (London: Wingate, 1957).

Fitzpatrick, David, *'Solitary and Wild': Frederick MacNeice and the Salvation of Ireland* (Dublin: Lilliput, 2012).

Forde, Frank, *'The Long Watch': The History of the Irish Mercantile Marine in World War Two* (Dublin, Gill and Macmillan, 1981).

Forster, E[dward] M[organ], *Abinger Harvest* (London: Edward Arnold, 1936).

Fountain, Gary and Peter Brazeau, *Remembering Elizabeth Bishop: An Oral Biography* (Amherst, MA: University of Massachusetts Press, 1994).

Fraser, G[raham] S[utherland], 'The Poetry of Consciousness', rev. of *Autumn Sequel: A Rhetorical Poem in XXVI Cantos* by Louis MacNeice (London: Faber, 1954), *Times Literary Supplement*, 2756 (26 November 1954), p.754.

Freeth, Peter, 'Nancy Spender at the Camden Institute', in *Nancy Sharp (Nancy Spender), 1909–2001 Memorial Exhibition: Paintings & Works on Paper* (London: The Estate of Nancy Spender, 2002), np.

'Further Fiction', *The Spectator*, 5448 (25 November 1932), p.30.

Gillis, Alan, '"Any Dark Saying": Louis MacNeice in the Nineteen Fifties', *Irish University Review*, 42:1 (2012), pp.105–23.

Girvin, Brian, *The Emergency: Neutral Ireland 1939–45* (London: Macmillan, 2006).

Greenblatt, Stephen, *The Swerve: How the World became Modern* (New York, NY: Norton, 2011).

Grigson, Geoffrey (ed.), *The Arts Today* (London: John Lane, 1935).

——— *A Skull in Salop and Other Poems* (Chester Springs, PA : Dufour, 1969).

——— *Recollections: Mainly of Writers and Artists* (London: Chatto and Windus, 1984).

Gwynn, Stephen, *Masters of English Literature* (London: Macmillan, 1904).

——— *Experiences of a Literary Man* (London: Butterworth, 1926).

Heaney, Seamus, *An Open Letter*, Field Day Pamphlet 2 (Derry: Field Day, 1983).

——— 'The Placeless Heaven: Another Look at Kavanagh', in *The Government of the Tongue: Selected Prose, 1978–1987* (London: Faber, 1988), pp.3–14.

——— 'Frontiers of Writing', in *The Redress of Poetry* (London: Faber, 1995), pp.186–203.

Herbert, George, *The Complete English Poems*, ed. John Tobin (London: Penguin, 2005).

Heuser, Alan, ed. 'Bibliography of Short Prose by Louis MacNeice (Corrected)', in *Selected Prose of Louis MacNeice*, ed. Alan Heuser (Oxford: Clarendon Press, 1990), pp.275–92.

——— *Selected Literary Criticism of Louis MacNeice* (Oxford: Clarendon Press, 1987).

——— *Selected Prose of Louis MacNeice* (Oxford: Clarendon Press, 1990).

Hewitt, John, *The Collected Poems of John Hewitt*, ed. Frank Ormsby (Belfast: Blackstaff, 1991).

Hicok, Bethany, 'Elizabeth Bishop's "Queer Birds": Vassar, "Con Spirito", and the Romance of Female Community', *Contemporary Literature,* 40:2 (summer, 1999), pp. 286–310.

Higgins, F[rederick] R[obert] and Louis MacNeice, 'Tendencies in Modern Poetry', *The Listener*, 22:550 (27 July 1939), pp.185–6.

Hilton, John, 'Louis MacNeice at Marlborough and Oxford' in Louis MacNeice, *The Strings Are False: An Unfinished Autobiography*, ed. E[ric] R[obertson] Dodds (London: Faber, 1965), pp.239–84.

Homer, *The Odyssey*, trans. Arthur T. Murray, rev. George E. Dimock, 2 vols, Loeb Classical Library 104 and 105 (Cambridge, MA: Harvard University Press, 1995).

'The Invention of the I: A Conversation with Paul Muldoon' [Paul Muldoon in conversation with Stan Rubin and Earl Ingersoll, 4 April 1996] *Michigan Quarterly Review*, 37:1 (winter 1996), pp.67–73.

James, Clive, *The Book of My Enemy: Collected Verse 1958–2003* (London: Picador, 2003).

[Johnson, Colton], 'Eleanor Clark', Vassar Encyclopedia, Distinguished Alumnae/i, <https://vcencyclopedia.vassar.edu/alumni/eleanor-clark.html>.

Keating, Frank, 'How Ravenhill rebels made an issue out of an anthem', Guardian Sports Blog, 26 February 2007, <http://www.theguardian.com/sport/2007/feb/27/comment.gdnsport3.

Kerrigan, John, 'The Ticking Fear', rev. of Louis MacNeice: *Collected Poems*, ed. Peter McDonald (London: Faber, 2007), Louis MacNeice: *Selected Poems*, ed. Michael Longley (London: Faber, 2007), *I Crossed the Minch* by Louis MacNeice (London: Polygon, 2007) and *The Strings Are False: An Unfinished Autobiography* by Louis MacNeice, ed. E[ric] R[obertson] Dodds (London: Faber, 2007), *London Review of Books,* 30:3 (7 February 2008), pp.15–18.

Kierkegaard, Søren, *Concept of Anxiety: A Simple Psychologically Orienting Deliberation on the Dogmatic Issue of Hereditary Sin*, ed. and trans. Reidar Thomte, Kierkegaard's Writings VIII (Princeton, NJ: Princeton University Press, 1981).

Kiernan, Frances , *Seeing Mary Plain: A Life of Mary McCarthy* (New York, NY: Norton, 2000).

Laird, Nick, 'Chianti in Khartoum', rev. of *Letters of Louis MacNeice*, ed. Jonathan Allison (London: Faber, 2010) *London Review of Books*, 33:5 (March 2011), pp.31–3.

——— 'The Seal and the Cat', in *Incorrigibly Plural: Louis MacNeice and His Legacy*, ed. Edna Longley and Fran Brearton (Manchester: Carcanet, 2012), pp.274–6.

Lear, Edward, *Laughable Lyrics. A Fourth Book of Nonsense Poems, Songs, Botany, Music, &c.* (London: 1877).

Lewis, R.W.B., 'Talk with Eleanor Clark', *The New York Times Book Review*, 16 October 1977, pp.11, 40–1.

Longley, Edna, 'Louis MacNeice: The Walls are Flowing', in *Across a Roaring Hill: The Protestant Imagination in Modern Ireland*, ed. Gerald Dawe and Edna Longley (Belfast: Blackstaff, 1985), pp.99–123.

——— 'The Whereabouts of Literature', in *Beyond Scotland: New Contexts for Twentieth-Century Scottish Literature*, ed. Gerard Carruthers, David Goldie and Alastair Renfrew (Amsterdam: Rodopi, 2004), pp.151–66.

——— and Fran Brearton (eds), *Incorrigibly Plural: Louis MacNeice and His Legacy* (Manchester: Carcanet, 2012).

Longley, Michael, 'Introduction', *Louis MacNeice: Poems Selected by Michael Longley* (London: Faber, 2001), pp.vii–xi.

Lowell, Robert, *Notebook* (London: Faber, 1970).

Lucretius [Titus Lucretius Carus], *On the Nature of Things*, trans. W. H. D. Rouse, rev. Martin F. Smith, Loeb Classical Library 181 (Cambridge, MA: Harvard University Press, 1975).

MacNeice, Dan, 'Rebecca', *Carrickfergus & District Historical Journal*, 7 (1993), p.51.

——— 'Memoirs', in *Incorrigibly Plural: Louis MacNeice and His Legacy*, ed. Edna Longley and Fran Brearton (Manchester: Carcanet, 2012), pp.25–41.

MacNeice, Hedli, 'The Story of the House that Louis Built', in *Studies on Louis MacNeice*, ed. Jacqueline Genet and Wynne Hellegouarc'h (Caen: Centre de Publications de l'Université de Caen, 1988), pp.9–10.

MacNeice, John Frederick, 'For Peace with Honour between North and South. An Address to Orangemen at a Special Service in the Parish Church, Carrickfergus, on Sunday 9th July 1922, Dedicated to Lady Frederick Cavendish' ([Carrickfergus: Bell[?], 1922]).

——— *Carrickfergus and its Contacts: Some Chapters in the History of Ulster* (London: Simpkin, Marshall; Belfast: Erskine Mayne, 1928).

——— *The Church of Ireland in Belfast* (Belfast: Mullan, 1931).

——— *Some Northern Churchmen and Some Notes on the Church in Belfast* (Belfast: Erskine Mayne; Dublin: Church of Ireland Printing and Publishing Company, 1934).

——— *Our First Loyalty* (Belfast: Erskine Mayne, 1937).

[———] 'The Care of Churchyards', in *United Diocese of Down and Connor and Dromore Year Book 1937* (Glasgow: Ecclesiastical Press, [1937]), np.

MacNeice, Louis, [as Louis Malone], *Roundabout Way* (London: Putnam's, 1932); repr. as 'Roundabout Way' by Louis MacNeice (London: Capuchin Classics, 2012).

———'A Comment', *New Verse,* 14 (April 1935), p.26.

——— *Poems* (London: Faber, 1935).

——— 'Some Notes on Mr Yeats' Plays', *New Verse*, 18 (December 1935), pp.7–9.

——— trans., *The Agamemnon of Aeschylus* (London: Faber, 1936).

——— *Out of the Picture* (London: Faber, 1937).

——— *Modern Poetry: A Personal Essay* (London: Oxford University Press, 1938).

——— *The Earth Compels* (London: Faber, 1938).

——— *Zoo* (London: Michael Joseph, 1938; repr. London: Faber, 2013).

——— *I Crossed the Minch* (London: Longmans, Green, 1938; repr. Edinburgh: Polygon, 2007).

——— *Poems 1925–1940* (New York, NY: Random House, 1940).

——— *The Last Ditch* (Dublin: Cuala Press, 1940).

——— *The Poetry of W.B. Yeats* (Oxford: Oxford University Press, 1941; repr. London: Faber, 1967).

——— *Meet the U.S. Army* (London: HMSO, 1943).

——— *Christopher Columbus: A Radio Play* (London: Faber, 1944).

——— *The Dark Tower and Other Radio Scripts* (London: Faber, 1947).

——— *The Sixpence that Rolled Away* (London: Faber, 1956).

——— *Astrology* (London: Aldus, 1964).

——— *The Strings Are False: An Unfinished Autobiography*, ed. E.R. Dodds (London: Faber, 1965); repr. London: Faber, 2007.

——— *Varieties of Parable* (Cambridge: Cambridge University Press, 1965).

——— *One for the Grave: A Modern Morality Play* (London: Faber, 1968).

——— *The Revenant: A Song-Cycle for Hedli Anderson* (Dublin: Cuala, 1975).

——— 'Recantation', *The Honest Ulsterman*, 73 (September 1983) pp.4–9.

——— *Collected Poems*, ed. Peter McDonald (London: Faber, 2007).

——— *The Classical Radio Plays*, ed. Amanda Wrigley and S[tephen] J. Harrison (Oxford: Oxford University Press, 2013).

——— Louis and Stephen Spender (eds), *Oxford Poetry 1929* (Oxford: Basil Blackwell, 1929).

Mahon, Derek, 'MacNeice in England and Ireland', in *Time Was Away*, ed. Terence Brown and Alec Reid (Dublin: Dolmen, 1974), pp.113–22.

———*Selected Poems* (Oldcastle: Gallery, 2000).

Manifold, Peter, 'Irish Responses to the Outbreak of the Spanish Civil War: A Comparative Approach to the Study of Irish Foreign Policy', unpub. PhD Diss., Dublin City University, Dublin, 2012.

Margetson, John, 'Nancy Spender', (Obituary), *The Guardian*, 25 June 2001, <http://www.theguardian.com/news/2001/jun/25/guardianobituaries.arts>.

Marsack, Robyn, *The Cave of Making: The Poetry of Louis MacNeice* (Oxford: Clarendon, 1982).

McDonald, Peter, 'The Fate of "Identity": John Hewitt, W. R. Rodgers and Louis MacNeice', *The Irish Review*, 12 (spring–summer, 1992), pp.72–86.

McDonald, William, 'Søren Kierkegaard', *The Stanford Encyclopedia of Philosophy* (winter 2014), ed. Edward N. Zalta, <http://plato.stanford.edu/archives/win2014/entries/kierkegaard/>.

McKinnon, William T., 'The Rector's Son', *The Honest Ulsterman*, 73 (September 1983) pp.34–54.

McWeeney, A. P[aul], 'Kyle's Genius the Highlight of Great Win over France', *Sunday Independent*, 25 January 1953, p.10.

Medley, Robert, interviewed by Andrew Lambirth, 'National Life Stories: Artists' Lives' (London: The British Library), <http://sounds.bl.uk/related-content/TRANSCRIPTS/021T-C0466X0019XX-ZZZZA0.pdf>.

Milligan, Spike, *Mussolini: His Part in My Downfall*, ed. Jack Hobbs. (London: Michael Joseph, 1978).

Morse, Samuel French, rev. of *The Earth Compels* by Louis MacNeice (London: Faber, 1938), *Poetry*, 53:5 (February 1939), pp.280–83.

'Nancy Spender', (obituary), *The Daily Telegraph*, Friday 24 July 2001, <http://www.telegraph.co.uk/news/obituaries/1310454/Nancy-Spender.html>.

Newman, John Henry, *Apologia Pro Vita Sua: Being a Reply to a Pamphlet Entitled 'What Then Does Dr Newman Mean?'* (London: 1864).

Nicholson, Elizabeth, 'Trees Were Green', in *Time Was Away: The World of Louis MacNeice*, ed. Terence Brown and Alec Reid (Dublin: Dolmen, 1974), pp.11–20.

O'Brien, Kate, *The Last of Summer* (London: Heinemann, 1943).

Ó Faracháin, Roibeárd, 'Some Early Days in Radio', in *Written on the Wind: Personal Memories of Irish Radio*, ed. Louis McRedmond (Dublin: Raidió Teilifís Éireann, 1976), pp.29–50.

Ormsby, Frank, *A Northern Spring* (Dublin: Gallery, 1986).

——— ed., *A Rage for Order: Poetry of the Northern Ireland Troubles* (Belfast: Blackstaff, 1992).

Orwell, George, 'Inside the Whale', in *Inside the Whale and Other Essays* (London: Gollancz, 1940), pp.131–88; repr. in *The Collected Essays, Journalism and Letters of George Orwell* Vol. 1, *An Age Like This: 1920–1940*, ed. Sonia Orwell and Ian Angus (London: Secker and Warburg, 1968), pp.493–526.

Owen, Wilfred, *Poems* (London: Chatto and Windus, 1920).

P.W.J., 'B.U.D.S.', rev. of performance 'Station Bell' by Louis MacNeice, *The Mermaid* (March 1937), p.71.

Pacey, Desmond, 'The Dance Above the Dazzling Wave', *Transactions of the Royal Society of Canada*, vol. iii, ser. iv (June 1965), pp.147–63.

Parsons, I[an] M. 'Mr. MacNeice's Poems', rev. of *Poems* by Louis MacNeice (London: Faber, 1935), *The Spectator*, 5597 (4 October 1935), pp.518–19.

Pickstock, Catherine, *Repetition and Identity: The Literary Agenda* (Oxford: Oxford University Press, 2013).

Plummer, Alfred, *An Exegetical Commentary of the Gospel According to S. Matthew* (London: Elliot Stock, 1910).

Poetry Foundation, The, 'Louis MacNeice', <http://www.poetryfoundation.org/bio/louis-macneice>.

Porter, Peter, 'The Achievement of Auden', *Sydney Studies in English*, 4 (1978) pp.73–113.

Powell, Anthony, *The Acceptance World,* Vol. 3 of *A Dance to the Music of Time* (London: Mandarin, 1991).

Quinn, Antoinette, *Patrick Kavanagh: A Biography* (Dublin: Gill and Macmillan, 2003).

R.J.S., 'Sir John Nicholson TD, MA, BM, BCH, FRCS', (obituary), *British Medical Journal,* 292 (29 March 1986), p.905.

Reid, Colin,*The Lost Ireland of Stephen Gwynn: Irish Constitutional Nationalism and Cultural Politics, 1864–1950* (Manchester: Manchester University Press, 2011).

Roberts, Michael [William Edward Roberts], 'Preface', in *New Signatures: Poems by Several Hands,* Hogarth Living Poets 24 (London: Hogarth Press, 1932), pp.7–20.

Rodgers, W[illiam] R[obert], *Irish Literary Portraits* (London: BBC, 1972).

Ronsely, Joseph, ed., *Denis Johnston, a Retrospective* Irish Literary Studies 8 (Gerrards Cross: Colin Smythe, 1981).

Royal Geographical Society, 'Michael Spender', Imaging Everest, <http://imagingeverest.rgs.org/Units/73.html>.

Rubin, Robert Alden, 'Some Heroic Discipline: William Butler Yeats and the *Oxford Book of Modern Verse*', unpub. PhD diss., University of North Carolina at Chapel Hill, 2011.

Scholes, Andrew, *The Church of Ireland and the Third Home Rule Bill* (Dublin: Irish Academic Press, 2010).

Sidnell, Michael J., 'Another "Death of Tragedy": Louis MacNeice's Translation of *Agamemnon* in the Context of his Work in the Theatre', in *Greek Tragedy and Its Legacy: Essays Presented to D.J. Conacher,* ed. D[esmond] j[ohn] Conacher, Martin Cropp, Elaine Fantham, and S[tephen] E. Scully. (Calgary: University of Calgary Press, 1986), pp.323–35.

Sorley, Charles, *Marlborough and Other Poems* (Cambridge: Cambridge University Press, 1916).

Spender, Philip, 'Introduction', in *Nancy Sharp (Nancy Spender), 1909–2001 Memorial Exhibition: Paintings & Works on Paper* (London: The Estate of Nancy Spender, 2002), np.

Spender, Stephen, *Poems* (London:Faber, 1933).

––– 'Poetry and the English', *Lilliput,* 9:6 (December 1941), pp.474–84.

Stallworthy, Jon, *Louis MacNeice* (London: Faber, 1995).

Starkie, Walter, 'Whither is Ireland Heading – Is it Fascism? Thoughts on the Irish Free State', in *Survey of Fascism Year Book* (Lausanne: International Fascist Organisation; London: Ernest Benn, 1928): pp.223–34.

Stephenson, Robert Louis, *Strange Case of Dr Jekyll and Mr Hyde* (London: 1886).

'St John Greer Ervine', CultureNorthernIreland, <http://www.culturenorthernireland.org/article/416/st-john-greer-ervine>.

St Leger, Alicia, 'Louis MacNeice: Poet, Writer and Broadcaster 1907–1963', Exhibition and Community Outreach Programme to accompany the exhibition at Carrickfergus Museum, September to December 2007 (Carrickfergus: Carrickfergus Borough, 2007).

Stuart, Francis, *The Wartime Broadcasts of Francis Stuart, 1942–1944*, ed. Brendan Barrington (Dublin: Lilliput, 2001).

Sutherland, John, *Stephen Spender: A Literary Life* (Oxford: Oxford University Press, 2005).

Symons, Julian, 'Louis MacNeice: The Artist as Everyman', *Poetry*, 56:11 (May 1940), pp.86–94.

The Tavistock and Portman NHS Foundation Trust, 'Our History, 1910s and 20s', <http://tavistockandportman.uk/sites/default/files/files/Our%20history_0.pdf>.

Temple, William, *Church and Nation, the Bishop Paddock Lectures for 1914-15, Delivered at the General Theological Seminary, New York* (London: Macmillan 1915).

———, *Christianity and the Social Order* (Harmondsworth: Penguin, 1941).

Thwaite, Anthony, 'For Louis MacNeice', *Times Literary Supplement*, 3706 (16 March 1973), p.292; repr. in *Time Was Away: The World of Louis MacNeice*, ed. Terence Brown and Alec Reid (Dublin: Dolmen, 1974), pp.111–12.

U2 (music) and Bono (words), 'Acrobat', 'Achtung Baby' [track 11], prod. Daniel Lanois, Island Records, 1991.

Unsworth, Barry, *Morality Play* (London: Hamish Hamilton, 1995).

Vance, Norman, *Irish Literature: A Social History* (Oxford: Oxford University Press, 1990).

Walker, Tom, 'MacNeice among his Irish Contemporaries: 1939 and 1945', in *The Oxford Handbook of Modern Irish Poetry*, ed. Fran Brearton and Alan Gillis (Oxford: Oxford University Press, 2012), pp.196–209.

Walton, J. Michael, 'Translation or Transubstantiation?', in *Agamemnon in Performance 458 BC to AD 2004*, ed. Fiona Macintosh, Pantelis Michelakis, Edith Hall and Oliver Taplin (Oxford: Oxford University Press, 2005), pp.189–206.

War Department, *Instructions for American Servicemen in Britain* (Washington, D.C., 1942; repr. Oxford: Bodleian Library, 1994).

Waugh, Evelyn, *Brideshead Revisited, The Sacred & Profane Memories of Captain Charles Ryder* (London: Chapman and Hall, 1945).

Welch, Robert, *The Abbey Theatre, 1899–1999: Form and Pressure* (Oxford: Oxford University Press, 1999).

Wills, Clair, 'The Aesthetics of Irish Neutrality during the Second World War', *boundary2*, 31:1 (spring 2004), pp.119–45.

——— *That Neutral Island: A Cultural History of Ireland during the Second World War* (London: Faber, 2007).

——— *The Best Are Leaving: Emigration and Post-War Irish Culture* (Cambridge: Cambridge University Press, 2015).

Woolf, Virginia, 'The Leaning Tower', *Folios of New Writing*, 2 (autumn 1940), pp.11–33; repr. in *Collected Essays* Vol. 2 (London: Hogarth, 1967), pp.162–81.

——— 'A Letter to a Young Poet', Hogarth Letters 8 (London: Hogarth, 1932); repr. in *The Death of the Moth, and Other Essays* (London: Hogarth, 1942) <http://ebooks. adelaide.edu.au/w/woolf/virginia/w91d/chapter25.html>; repr. in *Collected Essays*, ed. Andrew McNeillie Vol. 2 (London: Hogarth, 1986), pp.182–95.

Wroe, Nicholas, 'Nick Laird: A Life in Writing', *The Guardian*, 4 January 2013, <http:// www.theguardian.com/books/2013/jan/04/nick-laird-life-in-writing>.

Yeats, William Butler, 'Introduction', in *The Oxford Book of Modern Poetry 1892–1935* (Oxford: Oxford University Press, 1936), pp.v-xlii.

———*The Collected Letters of W. B. Yeats* Vol. 3, *1901 to 1904*, gen. ed., John Kelly, ed., John Kelly and Ronald Schuchard (Oxford: Oxford University Press, 1994).

——— and Dorothy Wellesley, *Letters on Poetry from W. B. Yeats to Dorothy Wellesley*, ed. Dorothy Wellesley (London: Oxford University Press, 1940).

Index